TENDER RETURNS

Other Books
in
New London Librarium's
Brazil Series

The Best Chronicles of Rubem Alves

Art of Love:
Paintings by Colleen Hennessy, Thoughts from Rubem Alves

Vertiginous Life

Miss Dollar: Stories by Machado de Assis

Ex Cathedra: Stories by Machado de Assis

Religions in Rio

Quilombo dos Palmares:
Brazil's Lost Nation of Fugitive Slaves

Law of the Jungle: Environmental Anarchy and
the Tenharim People of Amazonia

Journey on the Estrada Real:
Encounters in the Mountains of Brazil

Promised Land: A Nun's Struggle against Landlessness,
Lawlessness, Slavery, Injustice, Corruption, and
Environmental Devastation in Amazonia

TENDER RETURNS

Rubem Alves

translated by
Glenn Alan Cheney

New London Librarium

Tender Returns
by Rubem Alves
Foreword by Raquel Alves
Translated by Glenn Alan Cheney

Original title, *Retornos e Ternos*, was published by
Editora Papyrus, Campinas, S.P., Brazil.

Published by
New London Librarium
P.O. Box 284
Hanover, CT 06350
NLLibrarium.com

ISBNs
Paperback: 978-0-9982730-6-8
eBook: 978-0-9982730-7-5

PRINTED IN THE UNITED STATES

The thing that hath been, it is that which shall be;
and that which is done is that which shall be done:
and there is no new thing under the sun.
Ecclesiastes 1:9

This is the moment! Beginning at this door, a long and
eternal road dives into the past: behind us is an eternity!
Is it not true that all those who can walk
have had to walk down this road?

F. Nietzsche

… and the end of our journey will be to arrive at the
place where we started. And then to know it
for the first time.
T.S. Eliot

Contents

Foreword

Why is Rubem Alves so different and so special? That is a question I always ask myself. He is much more than a writer who wrote beautiful things. In the end, many write of beautiful things.

Memory is a strange phenomenon. It has its own will. It's like a dresser full of drawers with files inside. Everything is in its proper place, sometimes a little messy but within a logic that the heart understands. I say it has its own will because often I try so hard to open a drawer that just refuses to open. Other times, without my wish, the drawers open and the memories leap out at will. I have many memories of Rubem Alves as a father and as the simple human being that he was. And one day, in the middle of my thoughts, that's the drawer that opened, and suddenly the memory came to me in a scene all set up.

As a landscape architect, I have always been asked to reform, decorate, and design the gardens of my relatives' houses. My father, two years before passing away, wanted very much for me to fix up his apartment for him. It was an almost impossible mission. First, because a daughter is rarely heard the same way as a professional. And second, because my father had an immense collection of paintings and *objet d'art* that he loved very much. Satisfying the wishes of Rubem Alves by passing him through my professional sieve was a herculean puzzle. After painting the whole apartment and arranging all the furniture, my brother and I hung the paintings that he loved so much, with him staying with us, directing us, and approving. My daughter-architect's heart was happy when we finally arranged the aesthetic for all the things he had insisted on displaying. Finally he would be satisfied and stop complaining that his apartment wasn't as beautiful as he'd like. And I had the sensation of "mission accomplished," hoping that nothing would ever again leave its place...

A few days later I went to his office to give him a kiss, and I came across an old paper, wrinkled, tattered, stuck to the wall with glue! In an instant I stopped being rational and became furious. And he sweetly excused himself and explained, "I liked the scenery." I had only seen the wrinkled up paper and thought about the glue stuck to the wall. I had not noticed at all the scenery printed on it.

That is the reason Rubem Alves is so special. He

speaks to us about that which we would very much like to do but don't have the courage. I believe human beings are beautiful in their essence. Inside each is a soul that throbs and cries out for beauty. But we, swamped in the day-to-day, insist on looking more at the glue, the wrinkled paper, thinking about the wall. In reality, all of us would just like to look at the beautiful scenery and forget the rest.

A dollop of courage (and a lot of daring) is necessary to leave practical questions about the world of people on a secondary level and to choose the universe of beauty and sensibility, the one that makes our soul tingle as a point of departure. Rubem Alves, as a teacher who knew how to listen to his soul, dedicated himself to feeding it by only looking at the scenery.

I revere you as a man; I revere you as a father. You will be an eternal teacher. A teacher, so simple and beautiful, who touched the soul of humanity. You transformed into words that which was in your soul. That is how you managed to speak deeply into people's hearts.

In *Tender Returns*, his writing cracks away our hard, concrete layers and awakens in us a vision more sensitive to the life we breathe each moment.

RAQUEL ALVES
CAMPINAS, SP - BRAZIL

On Love

Go your way, eat your bread with joy,
and drink your wine with a merry heart...
Live joyfully with the wife you love
all the days of the life of your vanity...
Ecclesiastes 9:7-9

Love is the most joyous thing.
Love is the saddest thing.
Love is the thing I most want.
Adélia Prado

Friendship

$\mathcal{J}$remembered him and missed him. We hadn't seen each other in so long! With uncommon intensity I realized what a great thing friendship is. And at the same time it's the most joyous thing that life gives us. The beauty of poetry, of music, of nature, the delights of good food and drink lose their taste and become a little sad when we don't have a friend to share them with. I really think that everything in life can be summed up thus: the search for a friend, a struggle against loneliness.

I remembered a passage from Jean-Christophe that I read when I was young and have never forgotten.[1] Romain Rolland described his first experience with the friendship

---

1.   Jean-Christophe is the protagonist in three novels by French writer and Nobel Prize winner Romain Rolland.

of his adolescent hero. He had already known many people in the short years of his life. But what he experienced at that moment was different from everything he had felt before. The encounter happened suddenly, but it was as if they had been lifelong friends.

The experience of friendship seems to have its roots outside of time, in eternity. A friend is someone we've been with since always. The first time you're with someone, you don't feel the need to talk. The happiness of being together, one beside the other, is enough.

"Christophe returned alone through the night. His heart sang, 'I have a friend, I have a friend!' he didn't see anything. He didn't hear anything. He didn't think about anything else. He was dead tired and slept as soon as he lay down. But during the night he was awakened two or three times with a fixed idea. He repeated to himself: 'I have a friend,' and went back asleep."

Jean-Christophe understood the essence of friendship. A friend is that person in whose company it is not necessary to speak. There you have a test to know how many friends you have. If silence between you two causes anxiety, and when a topic fades away you go looking for words to fill the emptiness and keep the conversation alive, the person you're with isn't a friend. Because a friend is someone whose presence we look for not because of what you're going to do together, be it just talk, eat, play or make love. All that might even happen. But the difference is in that, then the person isn't a friend. Once the happy and lively activity

4

is done, along comes the silence and emptiness—which are intolerable. At that moment the other person turns into an inconvenience that clutters the space and whose leave-taking is awaited with eagerness.

With a friend it's different. You don't need to talk. The joy of being together is enough, one alongside the other. A friend is someone whose simple presence brings happiness independently of what you do or say. Friendship goes down paths that don't have plans.

An Oriental story tells of a solitary tree that could be seen high on a mountain. It hadn't always been like that. In times past, the mountain was covered with wonder—tall, graceful trees that lumberjacks cut and sold. But that one tree was crooked and couldn't be turned into lumber. It was useless for all purposes, so the lumberjacks left it there. Then came the gatherers of essences in search of aromatic wood. But the crooked tree had no aroma whatsoever. Of no value, it was left there. By being useless, it survived. Today, it is alone on the mountain. Travelers sit in its shade and rest.

Friends are like that tree. They live by their uselessness. They might be useful someday, but that's not what makes the friends. Their silent presence, useless and faithful, makes our solitude an experience of communion. With our friends, we know we are not alone. And there can be no greater happiness.

Love's Reasons

M ystics and those in love agree that love has no reason. Medieval mystic Ângelus Silésius said that it's like a rose: "The rose has no *why*. It blooms because it blooms."

Carlos Drummond repeated the same thing in his poem "The Non-reasons of Love." It's possible that it had been inspired by these same verses without his ever having read them since the causes of love are blowing in the wind. "I love you because I love you..."—non-reasons... "You don't need to be a lover or ever know how to be one."

My love does not depend on what you do for me. It doesn't grow from what you give me. If it were that way, it would flow with the power of your acts. It would have reason

7

and explanation. If some day I no longer have your gestures of love, it would die like a flower plucked from the earth.

"Love is a state of grace and is not paid with love." There is nothing more false than the popular Brazilian saying that "love is paid with love." Love isn't transacted with the logic of commercial exchange. I don't owe you anything. You don't owe me anything. Just as the rose blooms because it blooms, I love you because I love you.

"Love is given gratis. It is sown in the wind, in the waterfall, in the eclipse. Love escapes the dictionaries and various regulations... Love is not exchanged... Because love is love-nothing, happy and strong in itself."

Drummond had to have been in love to write those lines. Only people in love believe that love is that way, so without reasons. But I, perhaps for not being in love (which is a shame...), I suspect that my heart has regulations and dictionaries, and Pascal would support me because it was he who said that "the heart has reasons that reason itself does not know." It's not that the heart lacks reasons but that its reasons are written in an unknown language. Drummond himself was aware of these reasons written in a strange language and asked himself: "How can I decipher pictograms of ten thousand years ago if I don't know how to decipher my own interior? The essential truth is the unknown that resides in me and each morning punches me."

8

Could that be love—a punch from the unknown?

To the person in love, the deciphering of this language

is prohibited because if he understands it, the love will go away. Like in the story of Bluebeard: if the prohibited door is open, happiness is lost. That was how paradise was lost: when love—that fragile soap bubble—not content with its unconscious happiness, lets itself get bitten by the desire to know. Love doesn't know its happiness can exist only in ignorance of its reasons. Kierkegaard commented on the absurdity of asking lovers for explanations for their love. To that question they have only one answer: silence. But if asked to talk about their love without explaining it, they will talk for days without stopping...

But, as I've said, I am not in love. I look on love with suspicious eyes. I want to decipher its unknown language. Contrary to Drummond, I seek the hundred reasons for love...

I go to St. Augustine in search of wisdom. I re-read his Confessions, the text of an old man meditating over love without being in love. Possibly there one can find the most penetrating analysis of the reasons for love that has ever been written. And he confronts me with a question that no one who's in love would ever ask. "What is it that I love when I love my God?" Imagine if a person in love asked that question about his or her lover: "What is it that I love when I love you?" It might be the end of a love story. Because this question reveals a secret that no lover could ever stand: that to love the beloved, the lover is loving something that is not beloved. In the words of Hermann Hesse, "What we love is always a symbol." He concludes the impossibility of focusing your love on anything on earth.

Variations on the impossible question: I love you, yes, but it isn't actually you I love. I love some other mysterious thing that I don't know but which I seem to see flowing on your face. I love you because in your body some other thing is revealed. Your body is a lake where reflections swim like fugitive fish… Like Narcissus , I stand before it… "In the depth of your aqueous light my eyes swim in search…" (Cecília Meireles). That's why I love you, because of the enchanted fish…

But they are slippery, the fish. They flee. They get away. They hide. They make fun of me. They slip between my fingers. I embrace you to embrace that which flees me. When I have you, I'm happy in the illusion of having it. You are the place where I meet that other thing which, by pure grace, without reasons, came down over you as the Wind descended over the Blessed Virgin. But, by being grace, without reasons, in the same way that it came down, it can go away again. If that happens, I will give up loving you. And my search will begin anew…

That is the pain that no one in love can tolerate. Passion refuses to know that the face of the beloved (present) only suggests the dark objective of desire (absent). "Love begins as a metaphor," says Milan Kundera. "Or better: love begins at the moment in which a woman inscribes herself with a word in our poetic memory."

Now we have the key to understanding love's reasons: love is born, lives, and dies by the delicate power of the poetic image that lovers think they see in the face of the beloved…

The Stepmother and the Mirror

Snow White is a ditz, annoying in her silliness. The character that moves me for her tragedy is the Stepmother. If I could, I'd change the name of the story from Snow White and the Seven Dwarves to The Stepmother and the Mirror. Snow White is ditzy and silly to have not looked at herself in the mirror—she looked but didn't notice the terror and fascination that live inside it. If I like the Stepmother more it is precisely for this, because I have long conversations with my mirror—with my mirrors, because I have a lot.

Ah! You think this is stupidity, that mirrors are inoffensive objects of glass, cold and immovable, that do nothing but reflect images. Because that's right where your depth lies: in its ability to reflect. Jorge Luis Borges also has a fear of mirrors. He even says that they produce nightmares because two mirrors are enough to build a labyrinth. Try it yourself. Play with a couple of mirrors, one in front of the other, and see your face multiplied in infinite images.

You've never experienced the fright, in a restaurant or a house, to all of a sudden find yourself reflected in a mirror and see yourself as you wouldn't like to be seen, at an angle or in some weird way or even just in shame? Is that how I am? Edgar Allan Poe, according to Borges, felt the same thing. And in a work he was writing about the decoration of houses, he said that mirrors should be placed in such a way that no one sees themselves reflected without wanting to. The right place for the mirror is in the bathroom. Because when you go walking in that direction, you have time to prepare yourself with the certainty that we are whom we see in the mirror and not the one who sees us.

Which reminds me of a story from Gustavo Corção about an experience of his on, I believe, the elegant, bustling Ouvidor Street in Rio de Janeiro. He looked in the window of a bookstore and inside saw a gentleman with white hair, a familiar face which was staring at him. He respectfully nodded and tipped his hat with his right hand. And the familiar face did exactly the same thing at the same time, symmetrically except with the left hand...

Mirrors, according to ancient myths, are found to be linked with the origins of man. In the Sacred Scriptures it says that God created man and woman in his own image, reflections in which he could see himself. And the myth of Narcissus describes the tragedy of a man in love with

12

his own image reflected in a pool. And how he could never grasp the image, how it always disappeared as soon as his fingers touched the surface of the water, how he died of an impossible love.

The two stories relate to each other. In the first, it's God Himself who wants to see his image reflected... In the second it is said that what was sought in that reflection is the image of ourselves as beautiful that makes us able to love ourselves. The deepest desire of the human heart is that: that we be beautiful.

Fernando Pessoa came right out and said that he wanted to make a work of art out of himself. And he goes on to say, "Since I can't be a work of art in body, may I be a work of art in soul." Even St. Francis and all the saints, for all the mirrors they broke, just as the Stepmother did, they did it for the love of another mirror, the divine mirror where their hidden beauty could shine. That's why I like the Stepmother. In her I see my truth reflected. Because we are all in search of a mirror that tells us, "You are the most beautiful of them all!"

Ah! If we could find it, we would be eternally happy! When, on the other hand, as happened to the Stepmother, the beautiful image metamorphoses into an ugly image, we turn into evil witches and warlocks. We break the mirror, and poison spills over the body...

And that's how I think of love. We love people not for the beauty in them but for our own beauty reflected in them. What is a beautiful person? The one in whom we see ourselves as beautiful. When, on the other hand, the enchanted mirror shows us an ugly image, love leaves, and the mirror is either broken or is permanently put in a permanently dark room. We don't want to see it anymore.

Narcissus, I believe, is the most fundamental myth. More fundamental than Oedipus. Narcissus gives us the fundamental theme. Oedipus is a variation of it, a development. The story of the Stepmother and the Mirror is a combination of the two: first, a story of heavenly love, Stepmother and mirror. Love was found in the voice of the mirror that said: You are the fairest of them all." Later, the enchanting story is broken by the appearance of another, more beautiful, image. And the Stepmother suddenly sees herself excluded from the mirror. And she turns wicked. All exclusion does that. It awakens in us a cruel and ugly image, a dormant image that takes control of the body...

That's why we are beggars for looks. Looks are mirrors. Every encounter is a request: "Mirror, mirror, on the wall, tell me, is anyone in the world more beautiful than I?"

That's why we get prettied up, why we write, why we invite our friends to dinners, why we go to pleasant get-togethers with friends, why we do heroic acts, why we write poems, why we make gestures: they are all requests for recognition of our beauty.

Can you understand why I really do like the tragic figure of the Stepmother? Because she reveals the drama of love, its joy and its breakdown. We are all the Stepmother in search of a beautiful image...

The Thousand and One Nights

I am surrendering myself to the lazy pleasure of rereading *The Thousand and One Nights*. The enchantment starts with the title, which, in the words of Jorge Luis Borges, is one of the most beautiful in the world. According to him, its particular beauty is owed to the fact that the word *thousand* is, for us, almost synonymous with infinity. "To talk about a thousand nights is to talk about infinite nights (...). To say *a thousand and one nights* is to go beyond infinity."

The Thousand and One Nights is the story of a love—a love that never ends. Don't the immortal verses of Vinicius de Morães have room there (words so beautiful that the Devil himself used them in his argument with the Creator): "It may not be immortal, since it is a flame, but while it lasts, it's infinite." These are the words of someone who has felt the waft of wind inside that will soon blow that

15

candle out—a declaration of love that foretells a parting.

But that's what those who love cannot accept. Even those for whom the flame has gone out dream of hearing from someone, someday, the words that Heine wrote to a woman: "I will love you eternally and even afterward." The flame must never go out, even though the candle goes on consuming itself. The art of loving is the art of not letting the flame go out. You can't let the light sleep. You have to hasten to awaken it (Bachelard). And, a curious thing, the same flame that the wind so impetuously blows out returns to be lit again by the caress of a soft breath...

The Thousand and One Nights is a story of the struggle between the impetuous wind and the soft breath. It reveals the secret of love that never goes out.

A sultan, finding himself betrayed by the wife he loved madly, made a cruel decision. He couldn't live without the love of a woman. But he also couldn't stand the possibility of betrayal. So he decided that he would marry the most beautiful girls in all his lands. But, after the first night of love, he would have them beheaded. So each day love would be renewed in all the vigor of reckless fire, with no breath of infidelity to blow it out. The word spread across the kingdom that terrible things were happening in the royal palace. The young women were disappearing right after the nuptial night. Scheherazade, daughter of the vizier [who procured the young women] went to her father and told him her shocking decision: She wanted to become the sultan's wife. Her father, desperate, revealed to her the sad destiny that awaited her, since it was he himself who took care of the executions. But the young woman would not be dissuaded.

The way the story describes young Scheherazade is revealing. Almost nothing is said of her beauty. The story is silent on her erotic virtuosity. But it says that she read books of all kinds, that she had memorized a large number of poems and stories, that she knew by heart the popular proverbs and the dictums of philosophers.

And Scheherazade married the sultan. Performing the acts of physical love that took place on the nuptial nights, when the fire of carnal love had drained the body of her husband, when all that was left was to await the light of day so that the young woman could be sacrificed, she began to talk. She told stories. Her words penetrated the sultan's vaginal ears. Softly, like music. The ear is feminine, a space that waits and receives, that allows itself to be penetrated. Speech is masculine, something that grows and penetrates the spaces of the soul. According to an ancient tradition, that's how the human god was conceived—by the poetic breath of the divine Word penetrating the enchanted and receptive ears of a Virgin.

The body is a wonderful place of delights. But Scheherazade knew that all love built on the delights of the   *17* body has a short life. The flame goes out as soon as the body has emptied itself of its fire. Its sad fate is to be decapitated in the morning. In that it's a flame, it isn't eternal. So, when the flames of the body have gone out, Scheherazade blew softly. She spoke. She eroticized the sultan's dormant emptiness. She awakened the magical world of fantasy. Each story contained another inside itself, infinitely. There is no orgasm that puts an end to desire. And she looked beautiful to him as no other. Because a person is beautiful not for her beauty but for our beauty reflected in her...

As the story goes, the sultan, enchanted by Scheherazade's stories, kept putting off the execution for a thousand and one nights—eternity and one day more.

This isn't one love story among others. To the contrary, it is the story of the birth and life of love. Love lives on this subtle thread of conversation, swinging between the mouth and the ear. Sonia Braga, at the end of the documentary celebrating sixty years of Tom Jobim, said that Tom was a man whom all women would like to have. And she explained: "Because he is masculine and feminine at the same time...." The secret of love is an androgyne. All of us, men and women, are male and female at the same time. All you have to do is listen. Take in. Let the other come inside us. Listen in silence. Without expelling the other with argument or contradiction. Nothing is more fatal to love than a quick answer, a saber that decapitates.

There are very old people whose ears are still virgins. They were never penetrated. And it's necessary to know how to speak. Some speech is rape. The only ones who know how to speak are those who know how to make silence and how to listen—above all, those who dedicate themselves to the difficult art of guessing: guessing the dormant worlds that reside in the spaces of others.

The Thousand and One Nights is a story of each one of us. In each of us there lives a sultan. In each of us there lives a Scheherazade. Those who are dedicated to the subtle and delicious art of making love with the mouth and the ear (those sexual organs that I've never seen mentioned in books on sex education...) can be the hope that the mornings will never end with the wind that blows out the candle but with the breath that relights it.

Widows

With a hand gesture she motioned me off the couch where I was seated and called me over to the front window. The leaves and branches of an ivy covered the open space of the window, making it an ideal place for anyone wanting to watch without being seen. She pointed to three modest houses on the other side of the street.

"They are the widows' houses," she explained. "Not long ago death passed by, taking away three husbands. Now they are alone, three little widows in empty houses. The neighbors feel sorry for them and imagine how they must feel like those Sicilian women who, their husbands dead, cover themselves with sinister black clothes for the rest of their days so that everyone knows that their lives have ended. If they go on living, it's because religion doesn't let them put an end to their own lives. Nonetheless, they would like death to come soon..."

I stayed here at the window, looking at the closed

houses, imagining those poor creatures inside, alone, their only company sadness and longing... It was then that I began to notice signs of strange things happening in those three houses and in those three little old ladies. It happened after the passing of that period when, in fear of death, everybody feels the obligation to put on a sad face and speak only of the deceased's last moments. It happened after life had returned to normal and conversation turned light again... All of a sudden—so much so that it seemed like something imagined because it happened at the same time—the three little old women, whom everyone imagined to be dead, began to flourish. And they became beautiful like they'd never been, not even when their husbands were alive!

One of them, who had only worn her hair in a bun, cut and dyed her hair and even began to put on a little lipstick. She most certainly went back to talk with an old boyfriend—forgotten, abandoned, set aside, hushed—the mirror, which upon the death of her husband reappeared to say, "You don't need to be ugly anymore. he's gone. You are free to be as pretty as you always were..."

The second had always swept the sidewalk in her slippers, socks, and robe. She began to show up in the street in clothes of vivid colors that she had never worn before. Where had she gotten them? From some chest where they'd been lock up with mothballs, waiting for the big day? Or had they existed only in her chest of prohibited dreams that her husband had never let her open and which now flew free as butterflies released from their cocoons?

The third, of serious voice and no smile, spoke in monosyllable, and few can remember ever having seen a smile on her lips. Then, to the surprise of the whole neighborhood, she began to sing... She sang old songs of love, of other times—certainly from the times when she felt like a girlfriend...

The resurrection of these little old ladies made me smile with joy. But then I considered the tragedy of human life: It was necessary for death to do its work so that life could sprout anew. I remembered a terrible verse from Álvaro de Campos: "Perhaps it is worse for others that you exist rather than die...perhaps you weigh more enduring than to give up enduring..."

It's obvious that their innocent husbands knew nothing of this and knew nothing about the life that lay hidden under the weight of their presence. If they were able to revisit their homes, they would certainly have difficulty recognizing the women they'd lived with (or died with) all those years. Anyway, it was too late... What a shame that sometimes life has to wait so long to be reborn from the tomb! What a shame that sometimes, life has a chance only when death has done its job...

Until Death

Every once in a while the devil shows up, and we have long talks. In no way does he appear like they say: tail, horns, goat hooves, a smell of sulfur. A gentleman with a soft and rational voice, well dressed, a connoisseur of fine deodorants, he always surprises me with the logic of his arguments. No trivialities. He speaks only of the essential, a style he learned from God in the years when he was a disciple. I knew it was him when I noticed that he brought in his right hand the hammer, and in his left, the anvil. Because this is his mission: to hammer certainties, iron on iron, to see if they survive the test.

He was getting ready to deliver the first hammerings when I interrupted.

"What's that that you're going to hit? I think it's going to break into a thousand pieces…"

"The thing on the anvil looked to me like something made of pottery, a delicate, fragile figurine, and I was saddened that the devil was about to shatter it.

"I have no other alternative," he responded. "It's part of a bet I made with God. This delicate figurine is marriage. And you can be sure: it's not going to withstand the iron of my hammer!"

I was indignant that he had planned something so perverse.

"It's not for nothing that religious people say you are the anti-god. God unites. You separate. Your anvil has already destroyed many homes!"

He was in no hurry. He rested his hammer and with unperturbed voice said, "I'm used to such slander. But there is nothing farther from the truth. If there's anything I desire, it's a long-lasting marriage, until death do they separate. If I put marriage on the anvil, it's precisely to prove that the Creator's prescription doesn't work. Mine is much more efficient. What I say may sound strange, but you'd understand my reasoning if you listened to my story."

Since my silence indicated my willingness to hear him out, he continued to speak.

"Everybody knows that in the beginning, I was God's right hand. We agreed on everything. He ordered, I obeyed. It was over marriage that we parted ways. Until then, we'd worked together. When God said that it wasn't good for man to be alone, that it would be better if he had a woman, I agreed. When God said that this union would have to be without end, until death, I applauded. But then the bone of contention came up. To stick the man to the woman, God went to get the bread of love. I objected. I argued: 'Lord! Love is a weak thing, short-lived! Anyone stuck together by love soon separate!'

"I quoted the poet: 'May it not be immortal, in that it is a flame, but may it be infinite while it lasts!'" Love is a tenuous flame, a fire of straw. It can't be immortal. In the beginning, that enthusiasm. But it soon burns out. A candle flame, so weak that it blows out in any waft...Love is a ceramic figurine. All lovers know this, even those most impassioned. And is that not why they feel jealousy? Jealousy is the painful awareness that the love's object is not property. It can fly away at any moment. That's why love is painful. It's that whiff of uncertainty. The discrete touching of the hands, the soft meeting of the eyes: it's a delightful thing, no doubt about it. And that's why, for being so discrete, for being so soft, that love refuses to hold on. To love is to have a bird landed on a finger. Anyone with a bird landed on a finger knows that at any moment, it can fly away. How to build a long-lasting union with such weak glue? That's why couples break up, because of love under the illusion of another love. Any fool knows that the bird stays only if it's in a cage. Love is a glue too weak to produce a long-lasting marriage because within love lives the worst enemy of stability: freedom. The bird must learn that it is useless to flap its wings. A long-lasting marriage is the one where husband and wife lose their illusions of love.

"That's where we parted ways," he continued. "Not because we disagreed that marriage should be eternal.

That's what I want. We parted ways because we didn't agree on what joined a man and a woman eternally. God is a romantic. I am a realist."

Perplexed, I asked him, "What, then, was your proposal? What glue should be used?"

He smiled with confidence and answered, "Hatred. Anyone who thinks hatred separates is wrong. The truth is that hatred joins people together. As one of Guimarães Rosa's thugs, whoever hates someone takes that one to bed. Different from the flame of a candle, the flame of hate is like a volcano. it never goes out. From outside, it might seem dormant. Deep inside, the flames are crackling. The difference between the two? Love, due to its freedom, opens its hand and lets the other go. In love exists the permanent possibility of separation. But hatred holds it. Have no doubt: the most solid marriages are based on hatred. And do you know why hatred doesn't let go? Because it can't stand the dream of the other, to fly free and happy. Hatred builds cages, and there inside remain the two, gnawing on each other in a meat grinder that turns without stopping, each feeding on the unhappiness that can be caused for the other. People remain together to torture each other. Don't underestimate the power of sadism. Ah! The supreme happiness of making the other unhappy!"

That said, he took up his hammer and went back to work.

28

"I must prove that I, not God, am the one who knows the prescription for marriage that only death can break up."

I crossed myself three times and understood that hell is closer than I'd thought.

The Scene

Among the few books I have within reach on my bookshelf is the love story of Tomas and Tereza that Milan Kindera tells in *The Unbearable Lightness of Being*. Tomas had had many lovers. Of all his amorous adventures, "his memory only recorded the steep and narrow path of sexual conquest. All the rest (with an almost pedantic care) had been eliminated from his memory."

"Amorous adventures"? Tomas, in reality, had never been in love. His horror of love was such that he never allowed a woman to sleep in his apartment. The idea of waking up in the morning beside any woman bothered him so much that, once the sexual orgy was over, Tomas always found a way to take his partner back home. He seemed like the sultan in The Thousand and One Nights: After a night of carnal pleasures, the lover was decapitated... That's how Tomas saw himself, as an animal hunter who abandoned

29

his prey as soon as his hunger was satisfied.

But with Tereza, it had all been different. Not that Tereza had some special trait that set her apart from the others. No matter how much he examined her, he found nothing in her that he could point to as the reason for his love. Nevertheless, without reasons, the fact was, he was in love with her.

His adventure with Tereza had begun exactly where his adventures with other women ended. She had rolled out from the other side of the imperative that had driven him to conquest. He had met Tereza coincidentally in a little town. He said to her, almost like a game, that if she went to the capital, she should look him up. And he gave her his address. Tereza went and looked for him. She had arrived in the capital sick and didn't know where to go. That's how the love story began. She was burning with fever and slept on his living room couch, and he couldn't take her back home as he had done the others. Where could he take her? Kneeling at her head, "the idea occurred to him that she had come to him like a basket floating on the waters."

Now, from a distance, he thought about the reasons for his love, and he asked himself, without realizing it, St. Augustine's unusual question: "What is it that I love when I love Tereza?" Suddenly everything became clear. It was the beauty of this scene that he was in love with: Tereza, a frightened child, coming into his arms with a plea for help. Man can't resist the woman whose soul answers to his voice."

"It seems that there is a specific zone in the brain that we could call poetic memory, which records what enchants us, what moves us, what gives beauty to our life. As soon as Tomas knew Tereza, no other woman had the right to leave a mark, however ephemeral, in this zone of his brain."

Now, in his poetic memory, that scene remained immovable, imperturbable, out of time. It was a part of his soul. It would never die. Vinicius de Mores perceived that the love for a woman is not eternal, in that it is a flame. But he didn't perceive that the love of a beautiful scene remains forever, since "that which the memory loved remains eternal."

"What is it that I love when I love?" Tomas loved Tereza because beforehand he had loved something else: that beautiful and moving scene that suddenly shined in his imagination. The woman he loved was the Tereza of that scene: the frightened child who arrived in a basket on the waters." Tereza could leave him, get worse, or die. But the scene would remain unaltered, suspended in poetic memory as an object of love.

We love the beautiful scene before we love the person. That why St. Augustine said, in his Confessions, "Before I knew you I already loved you." We are lovers well before we meet a man or a woman who will be the object of our love. We are like a little child that loves an animal before first finding it. His or her poetic memory knows that it exists.

The soul is a collection of beautiful, dormant paintings, their faces wrapped in a shadow. Their beauty is sad and

31

nostalgic because, being dreams, residents of the soul, they don't exist on the outside. Once in a while, however, we are confronted with a face (or perhaps just a voice or a look or a gesture of the hand...) that without reason makes the beautiful scene awaken. And we are possessed of a certainty that this face that the eyes contemplate is the same that, in the painting, is hidden by the shadow. The body trembles. It is in love.

It happens, however, that there is nothing whatsoever the size of our love. Our hunger for beauty is too large. Neruda said that he was capable of devouring the entire universe. In the words of Adélia Prado, "for the desire of my heart, the sea is but a drop." And thus love reveals itself to be something sadder. Early or late, it will discover that the face isn't that one. And the beautiful scene will return to its condition of being an impossible dream of the soul. And the only thing thing left for it to do is feed on the longing that some face might satisfy.

Between Two Loves

*H*is heart was split between two loves. On one side,
an old love that fell apart and which he is now
disposing of. It had been attached to that woman for years
of gentle, tranquil affection, of real, sincere friendship.
Something must have wiped away that fact. During that
time, he felt like someone who walked on a colorful plain,
with neither mountains nor abysms, the air clear and free of
mist, knowing exactly what to expect. His love had reached
that state of certainty free of surprises, free of the sufferings
of jealousy and doubt that are hell for people in love. And
that's what he was leaving behind. And that's why he was
suffering.

He'd met another woman whose image, for reasons
he could not understand, awakened in the caverns of his
memory another scene full of mysteries, of exotic aromas,
of erotic shadows where the golden fruit of life grows.

33

And there, in this new scene reflected in the eyes of that woman, he saw himself as a different man with a young body endowed with wings, ready to fly over the unknown, a man in no way similar to the ruminating, domestic being who lived in the scene of the first love.

He'd fallen in love with another. He'd fallen in love with the beautiful scene that looked like a magical aura around that face. He'd fallen in love with his own image reflected in the other woman's gaze. He wanted to have her to be able to have himself in this intense way which he had never experienced.

He had to say good-bye. To leave behind the old faithful companion, the pallid scene, colorless and dull, that showed in her weary aura. That's how old loves are: faithful and weary.

But the idea of hurting her horrified him. To go to her and simply say, "I am in love with another woman. I'm leaving…"—that would be an indecency for which he would never forgive himself. He wanted to avoid the pain of seeing her left alone on the platform at the station as he departed.

The pain of the one who remains is always greater. It's like the pain after a burial, when you go back home and the space is filled with the presence of an absence. The truth is, the pain of departing is greater than the pain of death. Because death happens against one's will. He left me lovingly. He left sad to be leaving me. No joy is expected. That's why the thoughts of the one who is left behind rest tranquilly, without being bothered by fantasies of new loves and pleasures waiting for the deceased. Because nothing awaits.

Death can be the eternalization of love. Death firmly establishes the scene of beauty, while the departure destroys the scene of beauty. The person in love would suffer less with the death of the beloved than with his or her departure for a new love. Anyone who wants to understand the reasons behind crimes of passion will have to take that into consideration. Anyone who kills for love is like a photographer who wants to eternalize the beloved image in the scene of beauty. Isn't that what Cassiano Ricardo suggested in his poem, "Are You Your Picture?" he asks:

Why do I miss
you, in the picture,
even though the most recent?
And why does a simple picture,
more than you, move me,
more than if you yourself were here?

And after suggesting various answers, he makes the following statement: "Maybe because in the picture, you are immobile, without breath…"

You, alive, thankless, are the permanent possibility of surprise, the action that will destroy the beauty. But in the picture you remain motionless. You turn into a picture. Anyone who kills for love is a (cruel) photographer who immobilizes the scene. And thus puts it on the wall, like an object of longing and worship, forever. Roland Barthes said it well, that the only thing found fixed in a photograph, any

35

photograph, is death.

Yes, what to do? How to depart without making a good person suffer, someone for whom he'd had sincere affection? Sometimes a lie is the best way to go. There are cruel truths and kind lies. At the ethical crossroads between truth and kindness, may kindness triumph.

So he thought up a lie. He was going to say that he doubted whether she really loved him. Which sometimes he noticed in the faraway look, and that he imagined her distant thoughts walking among other loves. Which even, during sleep, she repeated several times the name of a man (Poor girl! She had no way to counter it. She'd been asleep...) So he wished the two of them could leave each other for a while. Be far apart, to see how it goes, so that feelings can become more clear. Distance is an excellent remedy for the confusions of love. And so that's what he did.

He calmly heard out her allegations without apparent disturbance. Once his speech was over, as he was getting ready to hear the counter-arguments that were sure to follow, what he heard was something else:

"You know your sensitivity keeps surprising me. How did you notice? I did everything to hide my feelings from you. I didn't want to hurt you! But now that you know, it's good to take on our truth. There is, in fact, someone else. The time has come to say good-bye..."

What happened at that instant he will never understand. Because those words were all he needed. He was free to give himself to his new love without guilt. But the only thing he felt was the immense pain of passion that all of a sudden exploded for that women who was telling him good-bye...

And he saw himself sad and alone on the platform of that station while she departed. The only thing for him to do was to go back to an empty house where no one was waiting for him..

As I said: It isn't the person we love; it's the scene.

Love Letters

I read and re-read a poem by Álvaro de Campos. I don't know whether I should believe it or doubt it. If I believe, I doubt. I doubt because I believe. Because it was he himself who said—or better, his other person, Fernando Pessoa—that he was a pretender. "All love letters are ridiculous. They wouldn't be love letters if they weren't ridiculous…"

In my office I have a reproduction of one of the most delightful paintings that I know of. *Woman in Blue Reading a Letter*, by Johannes Vermeer (1632-1675). A woman, standing, reads a letter. Her face is lit by the light of a window. Her eyes read what is written on that piece of paper that her hands hold, her mouth slightly open, almost in a smile. She's so absorbed that she doesn't even notice the chair at her side. She reads on foot. I think I'm capable of reconstructing the moments that preceded the one that the painter froze. Knocks at the door interrupt the household routine. She opens the door, and there's the mailman with a letter in his hand. By simply reading her name on the envelope, she knows who sent it. She takes the letter, and with that gesture she touches a distant hand. That's why love letters are written. Not to give news, not to tell anything, not to repeat things already known, but so that hands far apart touch each other by touching the same sheet of paper. Barthes cites these words of Goethe:

> *Why do I see myself once again compelled to write?*
> *It isn't necessary, my dear, to ask such an obvious*
> *question because, in truth, I have nothing to tell*
> *you. However, your hands will receive this paper...*

I return to Álvaro de Campos. Could this be the cause of the ridiculousness of love letters—the mismatch between what they say and that which they really want to do? Because the explicit purpose of a letter is to give news, and that's why they are made up of words. But what they really mean to accomplish is always above and beyond the written word. They want to accomplish that which separation prevents—a hug. Anyone who wants to try to understand a love letter through an analysis of the writing will always be off the mark because what it contains is that which isn't there, that which is absent. With any love letter, what matters isn't what's found written in it, only talk of desire, of the pain of absence, the longing to meet again.

That letter made everything stop. The woman closed the door and walked through the house without seeing anything, just looking for one thing, light, a place where the words would be illuminated. What difference does a chair make to her? She forgot that she's pregnant. Her eyes go over the words that came from the same hands that had hugged her. Her body is suspended in that magic moment of impossible affection that that little piece of paper opened in the time of her daily life.

A love letter is a paper that connects two lonelinesses. The woman is alone. If there are other people in the house, she's left them behind. It could very well be that the things written in the letter are no secret, that they can be told to everyone. But for it to be a love letter, it has to be read in solitude. As if the lover were saying, "I write so that you can be alone..." It is this act of solitary reading that establishes complicity. Because it was in loneliness that the letter was born. The love letter is an object the lover creates so the abandonment is tolerable.

I look at the sky. I see Alpha Centauri. The astronomers tell me that the star I see now is that star that was two years ago. Because that's the time that the light took to get to my eyes. What I see is that which no longer exists. And it would be useless for me to ask myself, "How is it now? Does it still exist?" I can get answers to these questions only two years from now, when its light reaches me. Its light is always late. I always see that which has already been... In this way letters are like stars. The letter that the woman has in her hands, which defines her moment of solitude, belongs to a moment that no longer exists. It says nothing about the present of the distant lover. Thus her pain. The lover who writes extends his arms to a moment that does not yet exist. The lover who reads extends her arms to a moment that no longer exists. The love letter is an embrace of space...

"It's good the phone exists," retort modern lovers who no longer have to live love in the space of absences. Mistake. A telephone call isn't a spoken letter because it lacks the essential. The silence of solitude, the calm of the pen poised over the table, waiting for and choosing thoughts and words. The telephone does away with solitude. In a telephone call we never say that which we would say in a letter. For example: "I was walking down the street when all of a sudden I saw a blossoming pink *ipê* tree that made me remember that time when...." Or "Re-reading Neruda's poems I found this one which I imagine you would like to read...."

The difference between a letter and a telephone is simple. The telephone is an imposition. The conversation has to happen right then. It lacks the essential element of the word that is said without expecting a response. And once it's over, the two lovers are left with empty hands.

But the woman has in her hands a letter. The letter is an object. If she had not been able to take it into her solitude, she would have been able to put it away in her pocket in the delicious expectancy of an opportune moment. A telephone call can't wait. The letter is patient. It stores its words. And after being read, it can be re-read. Or simply caressed. A letter against the face—could anything be as loving? A letter is more than a message. Even before being read, even inside its closed envelope, it has the quality of a sacrament: a palpable presence of invisible happiness...

These thoughts came to me after reading the letters of a young scientist, Albert Einstein, to his girlfriend, Mileva Maric. It was they that led me to the poem by Álvaro de Campos. They were ridiculous. All love letters are ridiculous. I think the editors thought the same. And as an excuse for their indiscreet act of making public something ridiculous that was a secret between two lovers, they wrote a long and erudite introduction that transformed the ludicrous love letters into documents of the history of science. They were worth something because, mixed in with the ridiculousness the lovers fed each other the editors found trails that give historians keys for the understanding of "the sources of the emotional and intellectual development of the correspondents." Not knowing what to do with (ridiculous) love, they put the letters into the archeology of science.

It was then that Vermeer's painting had me see the scene that letters hide. And the woman with a letter in her hand and a child in her womb? She might very well be Mileva, pregnant with an illegitimate daughter that was given up for adoption and about whom nothing is known. The child was given up. But the letters were kept. And for what reasons might a person have to keep ridiculous letters? Her absorbed face and half-open lips give us an answer. For those who love, ridiculous love letters are

43

always sublime. I return to Álvaro de Campos's poem and therein find what was needed to finish the scene: "but in the end, the only ridiculous things are creatures who have never written love letters."

An Illness without Cure

I would have preferred to be awakened by the crow of a rooster. Because rooster crows are more than rooster crows. Rooster crows are places where whole universes live, scenarios and times that might have been recognized by those who in some time past lived in them. Roosters are the heralds of a world. It would be good to hear them again because then I would return to those worlds where I lived and which are now infinitely distant in the past. To the opposite of the roosters are the *bem-te-vis* [great kiskadees, of the flycatcher family, *Pitangus sulphuratus*, that sings BEE-tee-WEE] that awaken me. From the tree in my backyard they announce the coming of a new day. And I admire the immense agreement that exists in them. They are all the same. Beginning with their uniforms. It's as if they were a party in which there are no dissidents. No desire to be different from what they are. And to judge by the convicted repetition of the same refrain—*bem-te-*

45

vi—it appears that they all have the same ideas. I've never known one to compose a different score. They are content. For centuries, millennia, they've been singing the same thing without tiring of it. The same inside and out. Which makes me suppose that they must be very good friends with each other since whoever is in such agreement can only be friends.

My fish cause the same admiration in me. For several months they have lived in the same aquarium. If I were one of them, I believe I would have long ago gone crazy with claustrophobia. Because the aquarium is a world without alternatives. There is no way out. Always the same things. However (which could be an equivocation on my part), they seem content. Contradicting the Sartrian maxim that hell is the other, they share the same limited space without any visible manifestation of either battles or insanity. I also image that, like the *bem-te-vis*, seeing each other so much, doing the same routines together, they must have become friends. In the end, all of them share one destiny from which they cannot flee.

Yesterday I found a dead *bem-te-vi* in the backyard. It was covered with ants. I found it by accident because nothing in the *bem-te-vi* song suggested to me that they'd been struck by death. The dead *bem-te-vi* was alone. None of the companions of the same uniform or same song expressed sadness. It was as if they felt no one missing at all. It was as if he had never existed! As if his song companions had never noticed him! There was no sadness in the air. No one missed his birdsong. He was just a *bem-*

te-vi with no name, like all the rest. Any other would be the same.

The same thing happened in the aquarium. A little red fish died. Just a day before he'd been playing with the other fish, swam in the same places, ate the same food. Now he floated inert on the surface of the water. But it was as if nothing had happened. The others didn't miss him. They continued their routines, indifferent, showing no suffering whatsoever.

When I was a boy in a small rural town, when somebody died, the churches sounded the funereal peals of the bells. It didn't matter if it was someone unknown. Everybody came to know that somewhere there was crying. A sacred space was opened—because that's what the sacred is: there where mankind cries together.

And I started thinking how we are different: the happiness of animals and the crying of mankind. Our bodies are different. The day goes on beautiful for the bem-te-vis, the aquarium goes on the same for the little fish, because—without their having learned this from any stoic philosopher—they naturally practice ataraxy, the absolute indifference to the blows of life. They don't feel. Or better, they only feel that which directly reaches their hide. Buddhism cautions us about that: that our tranquility is due to our desire. Eliminate desire, and suffering is reduced to pain felt by the body.

It so happens that the gods played with us and made our bodies out of another substance. In our flesh

47

lives desire. And desire is this: an opening to the whole universe, arms that embrace everything from the most distant stars to the infinitesimal creatures. Didn't Fernando Pessoa feel sorry for the stars? No, no he wasn't dealing in rhetorical symbols: he really suffered to see them shining sans surcease without ever resting. What good does it do to say that the stars don't feel if they live in the poet's body like a pulsing wound? One of my best friends—a friend at all times—is my dear John, a unique stonemason like no other. Every day, before beginning work, he goes to the edge of the swimming pool and saves all the little bugs that have fallen in—bees, wasps, beetles. Foolishness, they said. Because no one would miss bugs. They'll die anyway, and none of their friends are showing any feelings in the face of the tragedy of those who just yesterday were flying around with them. There will be other bees, other wasps, other beetles... Right. This is OK for animals. but it wasn't OK for dear John. His flesh, sick with tenderness, suffered from the suffering of little animals.

This is the sickness our bodies suffer: love. The skin is not its limit. It contains the whole universe. Pablo Neruda said: "I am an omnivore of all feelings, all beings... I would eat the whole earth. I would drink the whole sea." And our suffering is precisely that: Like a mother, we would like to shelter, protect, cherish everything that exists. And that's why the fate of a lost bird, a seagull covered with oil, a tree moaning as it's consumed by fire—these are internal tragedies that make our body tremble and cry.

I thought these things after trying to learn from animals

and plants the secret of their tranquility. And I concluded that this is a lesson that we are blocked from knowing. We will never be able to take part in their happiness. To be tranquil like trees and animals, we will need to have no heart. We are condemned to suffering because we are condemned to love. In the words of Wordsworth:

> *Thanks to the human heart by which we live,*
> *Thanks to its tenderness, its joys, and fears,*
> *To me the meanest flower that blows can give,*
> *Thoughts that do often lie too deep for tears.*

That is the price paid for having inside such a small body a heart that embraces such a large universe.

Tennis and Matkot

After much meditation on the topic, I have concluded that there are two kinds of marriage. There are those of the tennis type and those of the matkot type.[1] Marriages of the tennis type are a source of anger and resentment, and they always end badly. Marriages of the matkot type are a source of joy and have a chance at a long life.

Let me explain. To begin, an affirmation from Nietzsche, with whom I agree entirely. He said that, on thinking about the possibility of marriage, everyone should ask themselves this question: "Do you believe you will be capable of conversing with this person into old age?" Everything else in marriage is transitory, but the relations that challenge time are those built around the art of conversation.

---

1   Matkot is a popular beach game resembling beach tennis. It typically involves two or more people hitting a rubber ball back and forth with rackets, the object being to extend the volley as long as possible.

Scheherazade knew this. She knew that marriages based on the pleasures of the bed are always decapitated come morning, they end in separation because the pleasures of sex rapidly drain themselves and end in death, like in the Ogisa Noshima film *In the Realm of the Senses*. For that reason, when sex is dead in bed and love can no longer be spoken for through it, Scheherazade resuscitated it through the magic of the word. She started a long conversation, talk without end that would have to last a thousand and one nights. The sultan hushed and listened to her words as if they were music. The music of sounds or of words—it's sexuality in the form of eternity. It's love that always resuscitates after dying. There are caresses done with the body, and there are caresses done with words. And contrary to what inexperienced lovers think, caressing with words isn't all the time repeating "I love you, I love you..." Barthes warns: "Once that first confession has passed, 'I love you' doesn't say anything." And in talking, our true body shows itself not in anatomical nakedness but in poetic nakedness. Remember the wisdom of Adélia Prado: "The erotic is in the soul."

Tennis is a ferocious game. It's object is to defeat the adversary. And the adversary's defeat is revealed in his or her error: The opponent is incapable of returning the ball. Tennis is played to make the other err. The good player is the one who has the exact notion of her opponent's weak point, and it is exactly there that she tries to drive home her slice—a very suggestive word that indicates the sadistic objective, which is to slice, cut off, defeat. The pleasure of tennis is found, therefore, exactly at the moment in which the game can no longer go on because the adversary has been put out of play. It always ends with the happiness of one and the sadness of the other.

Matkot looks a lot like tennis: two players, two rackets, and a ball. But for the game to be good, neither of the two must lose. If the ball comes in a little out of line, the players know that it wasn't on purpose and make the greatest effort in the world to return it nicely, in the right place, so that the other person can get it. There's no adversary because there's no one to defeat. Here either the two win or nobody wins. And nobody becomes happy when the other errs—because the desire is that no one err. The error of one, in matkot, is like premature ejaculation: an unfortunate accident that shouldn't have happened since the pleasure is that back-and-forth, back-and-forth, back-and-forth... And the one who errs asks to be forgiven, and the one who caused the error feels blame. But it doesn't matter. The delightful game in which no one keeps score starts up again.

The ball. It's our fantasies, unrealities, dreams in the form of words. To converse is to be hitting a dream over here, a dream over there...

But there are couples who play with dreams as if playing tennis. They wait for the right moment for the slice. Camus noted in his diary of small fragments for books he intended to write. One of them, found in *Notebooks 1935-1945*, is about this game of tennis:

Scene: a husband, a wife, a choir. The first is worth

53

something and likes to shine. The second keeps her silence, but, with short, dry sentences, she destroys all the propositions of her dear husband. In this way she constantly establishes her superiority. The other dominates but suffers humiliation, and from that, hatred is born. Example: with a small, "don't be dumber than you already are, my friend." The choir cheers and chuckles at will. He blushes, comes to her, kisses her hand, whispering, "You're right, my dear." The situation is saved and the hatred builds.

Tennis is like that: The other person's dream is received so that it can be destroyed, burst like a soap bubble. What is sought is to be right, and what is won is a distancing. Here, whoever wins loses.

In matkot, it's different. The dream of the other person is a game that must be kept going because it is understood that, if it's a dream, its a delight from the heart. The good listener is that one who, when speaking, opens spaces where the soap bubbles can fly free. The ball goes back and forth…and love grows. No one wins so that they both can win. And so they wish that the other might live forever, eternally, so the game is never over.

On Wisdom

Let us be simple and calm,
Like the brooks and the trees,
And God love us by making us
Beautiful like the trees and brooks,
and give us unto the green of his spring,
And a river to have us when we're done!...
Alberto Caeiro

Fields and Scrub

I have a little piece of land in the Mantiqueira Mountains [in the region where Rio de Janeiro and Minas Gerais states meet]. I don't do anything with it. It's there as an object of pure pleasure the way it keeps being reborn each year from the mysterious forces of nature. I don't even need to be there to feel the pleasure of it. It's enough for me to think about it and know that it is waiting for me. Our eyes soon become fascinated by big things: mountains that go on and on until they disappear at the horizon, blue and hidden in mist. The creeks of clear water that run over rocks among ferns, to the songs of the swamp to the red flowers whose name I do not know, and which now and then turn into waterfalls. The giant araucaria pines, with their wrinkled trunks, paradises of red-necked woodpeckers and grosbeaks.

But my amazement is even greater when my eyes move

from the big things to the small, almost invisible things. The fields. You have to walk carefully, attentively, because beauty appears in hidden, unexpected places, and its size is so diminutive that it's all but unseen. It seems that nature ignores the distinctions we make between the large and small because its art is as perfect in one as in the other. There's the moss that grows on rotten wood with flowerings the color of squash. Carpets of soft green velvet in damp, shady places. Minuscule flowers in all kinds of shapes and colors in perfect symmetry: whites, purples, red, yellows, blues, violets, crosses, stars, suns, mini-orchids.

Scrub brush on a hill of poor soil. Tufts of sedge are highlights on the bald soil of the arid ground. Bushes with twisted, gnarled trunks grow, good for nothing. There's a line in Taoism that says, "The straight tree is the first to be cut." And it's true. Businessmen see tall, straight pine and soon start thinking that they can be turned into boards and money. But what to do with crooked, wrinkled trunks? Nothing. There among the crooked and wrinkled, the smell of wildflowers is delicious—the reason you can hear the buzzing of bees. And if your eyes are alert, they will discover bird nests hidden in the leaves. There are also wild fruits, among them the guabiroba with its taste of longing.

Animal life announces itself noisily in the chatter of moorhens, the cries of seriemas, the trills of finches, the gossiping of parrots, the croaking of frogs as evening falls. But most of all it's in the immense, surprising variety of invertebrates that nature seems to most delight, exhibiting its miniaturist art. There are minuscule spiders that weave their webs over the grass, umbrellas of transparent lace that appear covered with drops of dew in the morning. Every time I see one of them I stop, entranced, unable to understand how it is that such perfect art can exist without anything being taught or learned, in a body so small and alone. Butterflies, ladybugs, crickets, ants, ticks, bees, wasps, innumerable bugs that I see for the first time and whose name I do not know. All around each one of them, a wonderful universe that is theirs alone, incommunicable, in each body a dance, a symmetry, a beauty, a melody.

There's nothing to do about it, just enjoy. My thoughts become different. The head is like a cup that can be full or empty. If it's full of its own thoughts, all the wonders of the world are useless to it: it overflows like the water that overflows a cup already filled. To be able to see, you have to stop thinking.

Something Fernando Pessoa knew:

My eye is as clear as a sunflower.
I believe in the world as in a marigold,
because I see it. But I don't think about it,
because to think is to not understand...
The world wasn't made for us to think about it
(to think is to be sick in the eyes)
but for us to look at it and agree...

The world enters a soul when it's empty of thought. And thus we are invaded by its dance, its symmetry, its beauty, its melody. We feel happy. Happiness is an experience of fitting together, quite like that of the fitting together of

59

the bodies of people in love, in the act of love. In each of us resides an Emptiness that waits for something to fill it. We are all feminine. And when the Emptiness lets itself be penetrated by the beautiful, happiness happens. So, to know the soul, you just have to know the object that brings it happiness.

All the beauty and all the mystery of those fields in the Montiqueiras give me happiness because in some way they live inside me like a desire, like a longing for something missing. The whole universe lies dormant within our bodies. In the words of Hermann Hesse, "When we tarry in the contemplation of certain irrational, strange, rare forms of nature, a feeling of harmony is created between our intimate side and the force that willed these beings. It's that the same indivisible divinity operates within us and within nature. And if the outside world happened to disappear, any one of us would be able to recreate it because the mountain and the river, the tree and the leaf, root and the flower, every form that has inhabited the world is pre-formed within us, proceeding from the soul, whose existence is eternal, whose essence we do not know but nonetheless intimates to us as the innate power to love and the power to create energy and the power of longing for plentitude."

I've been advised to turn those useless fields into something productive. I've been told that the scrub brush should be burned so a forest of *pinus eliotis* can grow. It's been explained that this pine grows very fast and in a few years the trees can be cut and turned into good profit. I

walked through a forest of pinus eliotis. I was afraid. It was
dark. The silence is. Not a chirp of a bird. They don't go
there. I think they are afraid, too. The ground is covered
by a compacted layer of dry leaves. It's so compact that
not even a blade of grass can grow. And I started thinking
abut the crooked and wrinkled trees of the scrubby fields
and the life that lives in them. I thought about the fate of
those guabiroba fruits, the wildflowers, the bees… And I
concluded that my soul is a field of scrub brush, not a forest
of pinus eliotis. I've also been advised to burn the fields
and plant beans. "Beans are good money," they've argued.
But before I did that, I had to have a talk with those little,
almost invisible flowers, the little insects, the little birds,
the spiders and their webs. I did not have the courage. My
soul is a field as if it had come from the womb of mother
nature, but it isn't a productive plantation. To do as I was
advised was to turn a great and divine symphony into the
monotony of a samba of just one note… "Man does not live
by bread alone," say the holy scriptures. We need beauty,
we need mystery, we need the mystic feeling of harmony
with the nature from which we were born and to which we
return.

For as long as they depend on me, the fields will remain
there. As long as they depend on me, the scrub brush
will remain there. Because I am afraid that if they were
destroyed, my soul would be, too. I would become like the
forests of pinus, useful and dead. I would become like the
productive plantations, useful and empty of mystery. And
I asked myself if that's not what progress and education

61

are doing to our souls: turning the wild beauty that lives in us into the monotonous utility of monocultures. It's not to be admired that, with our hands turned toward wealth, an incurable sadness also moves ahead.

Lessons of Animals and Things

I envy plants and animals. They seem to me so calm, possessing a wisdom that we don't have. As if they were enjoying the happiness of Heaven. They suffer, for there is no life without suffering. But they also suffer as they should, at the right time, when suffering comes, not in anticipation of it. Knowing how to suffer is a hard lesson to learn. If the terrible hits us and we don't suffer, something is wrong. How to not cry if fate has made us bleed? If we don't cry, it's because our heart, too, is sick, having lost its capacity to feel. But to suffer at the wrong time is also sickness. It lets you get struck by blows that haven't happened and that only exist as phantasms of the imagination. Animals know how to suffer. We don't. We are prisoners of anxiety. Because anxiety is this: to suffer at the wrong time for a blow that, for now, exists only in a future we imagine.

Maybe animals are healthy of soul, and we are sick of soul. Norman O Brown, a dissident interpreters of psychoanalytic theory, seems to agree when he refers to the "simple health that animals enjoy but people don't." And Albert Caeiro calls plants themselves as witnesses to our illness. He says,

> *Ah,*
> *how the simplest of men*
> *are sick and confused and stupid*
> *at the foot of clear simplicity*
> *and health in the existence*
> *of trees and plants!*

And Jesus, suffering our pain for the suffering that anxiety puts in the future, advises us to learn from the wisdom of the birds of the sky and the songs of the fields, reconciled with life, living the pains and joys of the present, free of the phantasms of the anxious imagination. We suffer for the future and therefore we can't gather the modest but real joys that the present offers us. In a poetic document, mistakenly attributed to the elderly Borges (I'd like to have it in writing) these words of wisdom are found: I was one of those who never went anywhere without a thermometer, a hot water bottle, an umbrella, and a parachute. If I return to life, I would travel lighter. If I could return to life, I'd run more risks, travel more, contemplate more evenings, climb more mountains, swim more rivers. In case you didn't know, life is made of this, only moments. Don't miss one now. But, as you see, I am 85 years old and I know I am dying."

I think everyone knows, intuitively, that there's an insanity in the way humans exist. And that's why a nostalgia for a little farm or a house on the beach seems to be one of our most persistent dreams. Far from the yackety-yak of people where everyone's talking and nobody's listening, back to nature, where nothing is said and, in the silence, a forgotten wisdom can be heard.

They say that St. Francis preached sermons to animals. I don't believe it. I think they're wrong. Because the only ones who preach are those who believe themselves bearers of wisdom that others don't have. They preach to convince others to recognize their ways—to repent!—and so that through the words they hear, they become better. But of what error will they convince plants and animals? They are perfect in all they do. Butterflies and hummingbirds, wolves and buzzards, tigers and dolphins—they all act in harmony to the sound of the melody that plays inside their bodies. None of their acts is a lie. Inside and outside are the same thing. And what teaching do we have to improve them? So-called trained animals, the delight of circus visitors, only make me sad. They only learn what people have taught them to the extent that they forget that which nature taught them.

To the contrary, I believe that the saint conversed with animals, listened to their silence, and, if he said anything, it was as a pupil who repeats aloud that which he learned from his teachers. It wasn't the saint preaching to the animals; it was the animals who were teaching their wisdom. And maybe that's the reason why he is so loved. It's because in his acts and words he tells us about the plants and animals way of being, a way we have forgotten and which we would like to remember so we can be less unhappy.

St. Francis wasn't the only one. Zarathustra, according to poems that relate his life, tires of people and for ten years lived alone high on a mountain, his only companions an eagle and a snake. In the same way Thoreau abandoned civilization to live in the woods to learn something he wasn't finding in books or schools. And St. Augustine, in his Confessions, said that his teachers were things, plants, and animals:

> *I asked the land,*
> *the sea, the depth,*
> *and among animals the creatures that crawl,*
> *I asked the winds that blow*
> *and the beings covered by the sea.*
> *I asked the heavens, the sun, the moon, the stars*
> *and all the creatures around my flesh:*
> *My question was the look that I threw them.*
> *Their answer was their beauty.*

They tell me that plants and animals don't speak. Wrong. It's true that they are plunged into silence. But this is the silence that interrupts the cacophony of people so that one voice is heard, coming from the depths of our being. That's where our lost wisdom lies. You have difficulty hearing the voice of plants and animals? Read the poets, the prophets of their wordless wisdom. *Sugestão*, by Cecília Meireles, where she says that we ought to be like the flower that fulfills itself without question, the cicada, burning itself in music, the camel that chews its distant solitude, the bird that looks for the end of the world, the ox that goes to death in innocence. And she concludes: "Be thus—anything, serene, neutral, faithful. Not like the rest of men." With which Alberto Caeiro, disciple of the same teachers, agrees:

> *Let us be simple and calm,*
> *Like the brooks and the trees,*
> *And God love us by making us*
> *Beautiful like the trees and brooks,*
> *and give us unto the green of his spring,*
> *And a river to have us when we're done!...*

Gardens

After a long wait, I have managed, finally, to plant my garden. I had to wait a long time because gardens need earth to exist. But earth I did not have. What was mine was just a dream. I know that it's in dreams that gardens exist, before existing on the outside. A garden is a dream that became reality, a revelation of hidden inner truth, the naked soul offering itself to the delight of others with no shame whatsoever... But dreams, being beautiful things, are weak things. Alone, they can't do anything: birds without wings... They are like songs that are nothing until someone sings them; like seeds inside their little packages, waiting for someone to free them and plant them in earth. The dreams were living within me. They were my property. But the earth didn't belong to me.

The land was beside my house, tight, without space, between walls. It was vacant, full of trash, undergrowth, thorns, broken bottles, rusty cans, a place where fearsome rats lived, rats which once in a while visited us. When the dream closed in, I leaned a ladder on the wall and watched.

With my eyes I saw ugly things. With my nose I smelled its stink. It was what was there, a hard present "reality." But imagination is a magic thing. It has the power to see and smell that which is absent. So, thanks to its magic powers, I saw my absent garden and smelled its flowers and herbs. I thought that in some way, a similar things must have happened with God Almighty. Because the holy scriptures says that all around him there was only darkness and confusion. Things that made him sad. So he dreamed about a garden and understood that that was what would make him happy, if it existed. And he set himself to working to plant a Paradise. Work done, poems say, the Creator rested and gave himself over to pure pleasure. He saw that everything was very good. And, contrary to what the religious say (that he lives in the infinite sky, among the stars, among the angels...) he decided that there was no better place to live than in a garden. And there he stayed, taking special pleasure in passing among the plants in the warm breeze of the afternoon...

I didn't believe that my dream could be realized. I even went looking for another house to move to because it was certain that others had different plans for the land where my dreams lived. And if the dream of other people was realized, I would be like a caged bird, squeezed between two walls, condemned to unhappiness.

GARDENS

But one day the unexpected happened. The land became mine. My dream made love with the earth, and the garden was born.

I didn't call a landscaper. Landscapers are specialists in beautiful gardens, but that wasn't what I wanted. I wanted a garden that spoke. You didn't know that gardens speak? It's Guimarães Rosa who says this: "Many and millions are the gardens, and all the gardens speak. The birds of the winds of the sky—constantly bring messages. You still do not know. Always to the edge of the most beautiful. This is the Garden of Evanira. There might be, right now, another, a big garden with girls. Where a Little Girl, no front teeth, plays at being a Fairy... One day you will long for it... You, then, will know..." You have to long to know it. Only those who long understand the messages of the gardens. I didn't call a landscaper because, even if competent, he wouldn't be able to hear the messages that I heard. His longings weren't my longings. He might even make a garden more beautiful than mine. Landscapers are specialists in aesthetics: they take colors and shapes and construct scenes with plants in exterior spaces. Nature then reveals her exuberance in a splurge that overflows in variations that never end, in aromas that penetrate the body through invisible channels, in sounds of springs and leaves... The garden is a pleasing of the body. In it, nature shows herself as a lover... And how it is good!

But that's not quite what I wanted. I wanted the garden of my dreams, the one that existed inside me like a longing. What I was looking for wasn't the aesthetic of exterior spaces. It was the poetics of the interior spaces. I wanted to resuscitate the charm of gardens past, happiness past, joys already gone. "In search of lost time..." A person, commenting on the way I am, wrote, "Poor Rubem! He's become melancholic. From him you can't expect anything else..." He didn't understand. Melancholy is just the opposite: to go crying for lost joys, in permanent mourning, without hope of them being created again. To accept as the final word the verdict of reality, of the fallow land, the desert. Longing is the pain that is felt when the distance between dream and reality is perceived. More than that, it's to understand that happiness returns only when reality is transformed by dream, when dream transforms into reality. Now can you understand why a landscaper would be useless? To make my garden, he would have to be able to dream my dreams...

I dream about a garden. Everybody dreams about a garden. In every body, a paradise awaits... Nothing horrifies me more than science-fiction films where life happens among metals and electronics, space ships that navigate through the empty sidereal spaces... I'm left thinking about the derangement that led those people to abandon the forests, the springs, the fields, beaches, the mountains... Surely some devil made them forget the fundamental dreams of humanity. Surely their interior world also became metallic, electronic, sidereal and empty... And with that, the hope of Paradise was lost. As the Midieval mystic Ângelus Silésius says:

If, at your center
a Paradise you cannot find,
there is no chance of someday
entering it.

The little poem by Cecília Meireles enchants me. it's the summary of a cosmology, a condensed theology, a revelation of our place and fate.

In the mystery of the Endless,
hangs a planet.
And on the planet, a garden,
and, in the garden, a plot:
in the plot, a violet,
and on it, all day,
between the planet and the Endless,
the wing of a butterfly.

Metaphor: we are a butterfly. Our world, our destiny, is a garden.

Summary of a utopia. A plan for politics, for politics is this: the art of gardening applied to the interior world. All politicians should be gardeners. Or, who knows, the contrary: all gardeners should be politicians. Because there is only one political plan worth consideration. It can be summarized in the world of Bachelard: The universe has, beyond all the misery, a destiny of happiness. Man should re-encounter Paradise.

In Praise of Uselessness

I thought I knew my garden. Because it was from my head that it grew. Each plant had a reason to be, a history. A memory. Looking at it was enough to awaken in me my passion for gardening: beds to water, weeds to pull, earth to turn over, limbs to prune, pests to kill. Pruning clippers and trowel in hand, I was utility from head to foot. Work was necessary.

Then I got sick (that surgery, a while ago...) and all of a sudden the garden became different. I began to see things I'd never seen. They'd always been there, right under my nose. But I, utilitarian and in a hurry, had never seen them nor smelled them nor felt them. Pain obliged me to be a way I normally wasn't. Pain, when it's there, hammering, is an awful thing. The world ends, and it ends up being that place where the pain drills through. But there's another pain that stays off to the side, quiet, and says, "If you move, I will make you suffer...." Because this, my teacher, has taught me lessons, leaving me a little wiser. First, the lessons of humility, that feeling of absolute dependence that Schleiermacher identified as being the essence of religious sentiment. Before the mystery of life I can do nothing: I am alone. I am lonely.

Later, the virtue of patience. You have to know how to wait, because nature is slow. It still hasn't been reached by the insanity of rush. My plans for the day were forgotten, useless, with their lists of things to do and meetings to attend. With no pangs of conscience I felt the delightful feeling of not fulfilling a duty. To say *no* in a final and definitive way, leave the someone else speechless, with all the arguments that he had ready to convince me rendered futile. And, most important, it obliged me to do nothing. It taught me to live with, first, the affliction, and then with the delights of uselessness. I was unconcerned with my impotent, useless, dangling hands. Since I couldn't do anything, the only thing left was to contemplate, to receive.

There is a side of us that remains hidden, restrained, which only appears when we can't do anything. It's the receptive side, the pure pleasure of contemplation without trying to do anything. I just sat on the porch, watching. And the more I became at peace with my uselessness, the more the garden went into a striptease, showing me a nakedness

I had never seen.

First, the play of light on the leaves in the wind. The wind gusts, the leaves shake, forming configurations that never repeat. Since I couldn't do anything, the only thing left to do was be a spectator of the spectacle who says, "Very nice, encore, how beautiful!" And light, wind, and leaves thanked me and did a new dance.

I saw the shapes, the smooth and rugged trunks, thick and thin, solitary and branched, sunshade, lace, hearts, some dangling sad, other rising to the sky. Later, a curious dance from a hummingbird and a wasp, both seeking sugar water, disputing the same place. And the two of them became, for a moment, motionless in the air, one in front of the other, until the wasp, it seemed to me, recognized the hummingbird's rights and decided to withdraw.

I spotted the place where the waxbills had built a nest. I'd already heard their chirping several times, but I hadn't had time to see them disappear into the leaves of the bougainvilleas.

And the buzzards, wonderfully beautiful in the depths of the sky, not a single movement to disturb the peacefulness of their harmony with the wind. I also thought about the invisible movement of the vital fluids running through the plants, vegetal blood, silent manifestation of the mystery of life. And I accompanied the changes in the spirit of time. I heard the secrets of the mornings (joyous), midday (stopped) and afternoons (sad).

It was in the middle of this guiltless uselessness that I gave in to the luxury of books that for a long time had been awaiting me on the shelf. The to-do lists of important things (!) had obliged me to leave them for later. But now I was no longer something useful. I couldn't be used for anything. I enjoyed the supreme freedom of being absolutely useless and could hand myself over to the daydreams of thought without anyone demanding anything from me. I began with the heavy books. I got tired. I moved on to others, lighter, and finally I voraciously gave in to the supreme form of uselessness: I began to read Agatha Christie. I forgot everything because all mysteries are the same and end the same way. But I didn't forget one page. The characters were discussing a painting of an old Chinese man absently involved in a game with strings. And someone commented, "You have to be very wise to be able to do nothing!" And I envied the old Chinese. I wasn't playing with strings, but the mystery books were still a spool of threads that needed to be untangled. I loved the old, unknown man, and I thought that maybe this is what we need to learn: to be less crazy and a little more wise, that there is a supreme form of happiness that we can enjoy only when we surrender to the delightful irresponsibility of uselessness. I liked the idea so much that I'm even going to write about it again.

Doing Nothing

The morning is the way I like it. Blue sky, cool breeze. Soon, still early, it invites me to do nothing. Take a walk—not for reasons of health but for pure pleasure. The pink *ipê* trees have blossomed before their time—have you noticed? And there's nothing more beautiful than the crown of an *ipê* tree against a blue sky. All anxious thoughts stop, and you become possessed by the pure thankfulness that life is so generous with beautiful things. There, under the *ipê*, there's nothing I have to do. There's nothing I should do. Any action on my part would be superfluous. Because how could I improve that which is perfect?

I remember my first lessons in philosophy, how I laughed when I read that, for Taoism, supreme happiness is that to which they give the name *Wu-Wei*—to do nothing. I thought they were crazy. Because in those days, I was an ethical being who judged that action was the most important thing. I still haven't learned the lessons of Paradise—that when we are before beauty, the only thing for us to do…is nothing, to enjoy the happiness that it offers us.

I wanted to ask the *ipê* trees the reason behind their ambivalence. Could it be, perchance, that they had no agenda? Because if they did, they would know that the blossoming of the *ipê* is scheduled only for the month of July. Anyone who pays attention to nature's seasons knows that. But, before I could ask my stupid question, I heard, inside myself, the answer they would have given me. They would have answered by citing the medieval mystic Angelus Silesius, who said that flowers have no why; they bloom because they bloom. I thought it would be good if we, too, were like plants, if our actions were a pure overflowing of vitality, a pure explosion of beauty that grew from within and could no longer be contained. Without why, for pure pleasure.

But now I look at the table, and a book with a green cover reminds me that I don't live in Paradise, that I don't have the right to live for pleasure. What everyone asks of me isn't that I blossom like the *ipês* but that I fulfill my obligations—even though they take me a bit distant from my happiness. For obligation is this: that voice that shouts louder than my unborn flowers—my desires—and obliges me to do what I don't want. Because if I wanted to, it wouldn't need to shout. I would do it for pure pleasure. And if it shouts to obligate me to obey, it's because that which duty demands isn't that which the soul requests. Given that, look at the wisdom of two lines from Fernando Pessoa. First, the one where he says, "Ah, the lushness in the face of not fulfilling a duty!" Shameless, irresponsible, corruptor of youth, ought to be forced to drink hemlock like Socrates! It's none of that. It only tells the truth: we can be happy only when we are like the *ipês*, when we bloom because we bloom; when no one tells us what to do and what we are doing is only a child of pleasure. And the other verse, the one where he says that we are in the gap between what we desire and what others desire from us.

In my book with the green cover are written the desires of others. It is called an agenda. My own desires do not need reminders from anybody. They don't need to be written down. I know them by heart (yes, in my breast). By heart means in the heart.

That which is written in the heart does not need agendas because we don't forget it. Whatever the memory loves remains forever. If I need an agenda it's because it's not in my heart. It isn't my desire. It's the desire of someone else. My schedule tells me that I should leave my conversation with the *ipês* for later because there are duties to be done. And that I should remember the first lesson in morals administered to any child: first your duties, then your devotion; first the agenda, then the pleasure; first the desires of others, then your own desires. Isn't that the basis of all social life? A good, responsible person isn't the one who forgets his or her desires and obeys the desires of someone else—never minding that the other person lives inside himself or herself?

Ah! Many people have no soul. What they have in

its place is an agenda. That's why they are incapable of understanding what I'm saying. In their agenda-souls there is no place for desire. In the place of the *ipês* there is only an immense emptiness. There's an emptiness that is good: emptiness of hunger (which leaves a place for desire to eat); the emptiness of cupped hands (which makes a place where water can fall from the spigot); the emptiness of arms (which makes a place for a hug); the emptiness of longing (which makes a place for happiness to return).

But there's an emptiness that doesn't make a place for anything, a deserted-emptiness, a desert where demons live. And this emptiness, the tomb of desire, needs to be filled in some way. Because if it isn't, anxiety will come to live there.

Anxiety is a hole left by forgotten desire, the hole of a heart that no longer exists, a desperate shout asking for desire and the heart to come back so that the beauty of the crown of the *ipê* against the blue sky can be enjoyed. This emptiness is so terrible that various rituals have been created to exorcise the demons that live in it. One of them is my agenda—and the agenda of the whole world. When anxiety arrives, just reading the written instructions is enough. The hole is filled with commands and becomes an illusion that all is well. And is that why so much work gets done—from housewives sweeping homes to the stock market of businessmen? They are all the same. They all struggle against the same fear of emptiness.

And you, for whom life is furious work and restlessness—are you not weary of living? Are you not ripe for death's preaching? All of you for whom furious work is something dear—and also all that is fast, new and different—you find it too hard to bear yourselves; your industriousness is an escape, a desire to forget yourselves. You do not have enough space inside yourselves to wait—not even for idleness. (Nietzsche) That's why we turn on televisions—to fill the emptiness.

That's why we spend Sunday reading newspapers (even while our children are playing on the see-saw at the park)—to fill the emptiness. That's why we can't stand the idea of an idle weekend without doing something. (And on Monday asking ourselves, "And next weekend, what are we going to do?") That's why even on the beach we fill ourselves with frenetic business—because we are afraid of the thoughts that might visit us in the calm of contemplating the sea, which never tires of doing the same thing.

The Taoists are right: supreme happiness is the *Wu-Wei* of doing nothing. Because only those who are at peace with life can receive the delights of contemplation and not forget their own desires.

The Essential Things

ead this poem good and slow, as each image deserves
a lazy look:

In the mystery of the Endless,
hangs a planet.
And on the planet, a garden,
and, in the garden, a plot:
in the plot, a violet,
and on it, all day,
between the planet and the Endless,
the wing of a butterfly.

It's short, but it says everything. Nothing is missing. Uni-verse. No words could be added to it. No word could be taken out. That's how a poem is made, with essential words. The poem says the essential.

The essential is that which, if it were stolen, we would die. That which cannot be forgotten. The substance of our body and our soul. That's why people commit suicide: when they feel robbed of the essential, mutilated beyond remedy, and so life is no longer worth living.

Poets are those who, in the middle of ten thousand things that distract us, are capable of seeing the essential and call it by name. When that happens, the heart smiles and feels at peace. It found what it was looking for. This is how Kirilov, a character from Dostoyevski, describes finding the essential: "There are moments when you suddenly feel the presence of eternal harmony. It's a clear, unarguable, absolute feeling. We suddenly grab the whole of nature and we say that's exactly how it is! Its such a great joy! If it lasted more than five seconds, the soul would not stand it and would have to disappear. In these five seconds I live an entire experience, and I would give my entire life for them. They are worth it."

Her name was Norma. She was sick, very sick. On the eve of her death, she dragged herself to the bathroom and got to the sink to wash the vomit off herself. She opened the faucet and cold water ran over her hands... She stopped as if enchanted by the liquid that caressed her. And from her mouth came these unexpected words: "Water... How it is beautiful! Whenever I think of it, I think of God. I think God is like that...."

Death in the sink.

Water that slides

Eyes that contemplate eternity...

Norma's essential universe is full of fresh springs and

clear brooks where her hands play.

The name of the film I do not remember. I know it was being shown in Japan. An old married couple. The wife had died. The children came together to divide up the things she left. All of a sudden they noticed an absence. Their father, where was he? He wasn't there with them. After a long, painful wait, along he came, his figure bathed in crepuscular light.

"Father, where did you go? We were worried!"

"Where did I go? I went to see the sunset...It's so beautiful..."

The children divided the spoils.

Their father's eyes contemplated the colorful horizon...

The father's essential universe is full of sunsets. Without them, his eyes would be eternally sad...

This poem is by Brecht:

> *When in the white room at the Charité [hospital],*
> *I awoke one morning*
> *and heard the blackbird, I understood*
> *Better. For some time*
> *I had lost all fear of death. For nothing*
> *Can be wrong with me if I myself*
> *Am nothing. Now*
> *I managed to enjoy*
> *The song of every blackbird after me...*

White death in a hospital room,
outside, a blackbird sings.

Happiness from songs I will not hear.

In Brecht's essential universe, the song of blackbirds will continue without end.

I ask if, after navigating,
someplace, finally arriving...
What will be even sadder.
Neither ship nor gull: only uber-humans
companies...

Cecília Meireles knew what was essential. In her world, ships sailed the waters and seagulls soared the skies...

What is the essential? The ancient philosophers reduced the essential to four fundamental elements: water, earth, air, fire. I agree with them. They thought they were doing cosmology but they were doing poetry. They knew the secrets of the soul. That is what we are made of. I can imagine a world without wonders of technology without feeling any special sadness. But I can't think of a world without falling rain, without crystal-clear brooks, without the mysterious sea... I cannot imagine a world without the heat of the sun that pleases the skin and colors the dust, without fire that illuminates and warms... I cannot imagine a world without wind where the clouds sail, the birds, and the smell of magnolias... I cannot imagine a world without the earth pregnant with life where plants sink their roots... These are the lovers life makes love with and makes pregnant, where all the exuberance and mystery of the world, our home, sprout. I need no gods more beautiful than these.

THE ESSENTIAL THINGS

I hear, throughout the world amid the noise of ten thousand things that make up our insanity, the voice-poems of those who perceive the essential. They say just one thing: "This wonderful world needs to be preserved." But I also hear the dark voice of those who ask, 'Can we do it?"

On Princes and Frogs

*M*any, many years ago, before asphalt, when the Fernão Dias Highway was either a sea of dust or a sea of mud, trips were adventures. I lived in a rural area of Minas Gerais, and the way to come to Campinas to see my girlfriend was to arrange a ride in some truck. One of those times the driver, delicately, to begin a conversation that promised to be very long, asked me, "What do you do?" I could have answered simply, 'I'm a professor." This he would understand perfectly well since he had gone to schools, knew a lot about professors, and would have gone on to tell about his accomplishments in arithmetic and his difficulties with his native tongue. But I, foolish and inexperienced, and to give myself an air of importance, answered, "I am a professor of philosophy..." The driver's face lit up in a wide smile. "At last," he said. "For so many years I've been wanting to know what philosophy is and until today I haven't found anyone who can explain it to me. But today I have the fortune of having a professor of philosophy as a travel mate. Today I will have the explanation. When you come right down to it, what is philosophy?

I have no memory whatsoever of what I told him in my useless explanation. But his smile comes back to me whenever I reveal to someone that I am a psychoanalyst. Because inevitably the same question comes up: "What is a psychoanalyst?" The wisest ones, who have already heard of or read about the subject, dispense with introductions and go on to examine the issues. "And what line do you follow?" It makes me want to say I prefer curved lines to straight lines—which would not be faithful to the spirit of psychoanalysis, where the curve is always the shortest distance between two points. but I know they would not understand because what they want to know is whether I am a Freudian, Kleinian, Bionian, Jungian, Lacanian, etc. It so happens that's not my way. Preferring curved lines to straight lines, I follow the counsel of Guimarães Roa: I only give answers to questions that no one ever asked. So, half in an oriental style, half in an evangelical style, I tell a story:

"Once upon a time there was a prince with a wonderful voice who sang to all the creatures that would listen to him. His song was so beautiful that he even seduced the witch who lived in the black forest and with whom he, too, fell in love. But, different from the other listeners, who felt happy just to listen, she decided to sing, too. What a lovely duet we will make, she thought. And she set herself to singing. As it happens, however, witches never manage to sing very well. As soon as she opened her mouth, the most bizarre sounds came forth. They soared like the toads and frogs. The booing was everywhere. The witch filled with crazed envy and cast on him the most terrible of spells: If I cannot sing as you sing, then I will have you sing as I sing! And the prince was turned into a toad. Ashamed of his new form, he fled and hid in the bottom of a swamp, where he lived with the toads and frogs. In every way he looked like the batrachians. Except for one thing. He continued to sing as beautifully as ever. But now the ones who didn't like the singing of the new toad were the toads and frogs who only knew how to croak. The new song soared around their ears like something from another world, which disturbed the harmony of their monotone marsh. They sternly warned him, whoever lives with frogs and toads must croak like frogs and toads. The toad-prince stopped singing and had no other choice: he had to learn to croak as all the others did. And he repeated it so much that he ended up forgetting songs of the past. No, no…he didn't forget… Because when he slept, he remembered and heard the old, prohibited music singing inside him. But when he awoke, he forgot. But not everything. He had an undefinable longing. Longing for he didn't know what. Longing that told him that he was far, far away from home…"

That is a summary of psychoanalysis, as I understand it. It's a story that is mixed with love, beauty, and spells of forgetting. Do you feel fooled? You were expecting famous names, complicated concepts—and instead I told a fairy tale. Words to put children to sleep, they said. But I reply: It's to make adults wake up…. Psychoanalysis is a struggle

93

to break the spell of the bad word that puts us to sleep and makes us forget the beautiful melody. It's an attentive listen to a song that can be heard only in the intervals of silence in the croaking of frogs, and that comes to us like fleeting little disconnected fragments. It's a battle to make us retake the destiny written in the depths of the sea of the soul.

I've read the classics. But it was from the words of anonymous tellers of stories of enchantment and of the enchantment of the word of poets in which dead words become living things. Fernando Pessoa tells these secrets of body and soul better than I. Read these lines. But read slowly. Read them again. He is speaking of our mystery. It is our mystery that he invokes:

> *Cease your song!*
> *Cease, for, while I listened,*
> *I have heard another voice*
> *coming as if in interstices*
> *of the soft charm*
> *as if your song came to us.*
> *I heard you and heard it*
> *at the same time and different*
> *to sing together.*
> *And the song that wasn't,*
> *if now remembering it, makes me cry.*

And he asks:

> *Was it your enchantment voice which,*
> *unwilling, at this vague moment*

awakened some alien being that spoke to us?

Could that be it? Some other being lives inside us? In the interstices of croaking, a song? What other being is that?

What angel, as you raise your voice,
without your knowing,
comes down over this earth where the soul wanders,
and with his wings fans the embers of an unknown
hearth?

Living inside us an other who does not forget our truth...

Some think that psychoanalysis and poetry are the stuff of the insane. There's even a saying: *Everyone has a grain of the poet and the insane.* The toads and the frogs, hearing the songs of the poet prince, must have said: *He's a poet! He's crazy!* And tried to cure him, educating him on reality. For them, to be normal is to croak as everybody else croaks. But the soul, in the middle of the noisy monotone of life, continues to heave a voice in the intervals. It continues to cry when it hears a melody that wasn't there. It continues to hear the talk of an alien that lives within us and visits us in our dreams.

He continues to be burned by the embers of longing for a forgotten hearthstone from which we are exiled.

It is quite possible that toads and frogs live more tranquilly. For them, all the issues have been resolved.

But there is a happiness that resides only in beauty. And this we find only in the song that soars, forgotten and repressed in the bottom of the soul.

On Calamities

There are calamities in life, so strong…I don't know. Calamities as if from God's hatred; as if before them, the repercussion of everything suffered settles in the soul… I don't know! And man…Poor man…poor man! He turns his eyes, and everything he's lived settles, as if in a swamp of guilt, within sight.

Cesar Vallejo

Between the Hammer and the Anvil

They talk bad about the Devil. I've concluded that this is unfair, a badmouthing. I've been talking with him, and from the thoughts that he made me think, I came to the conclusion that he isn't the villain that everyone says...

It all began in the hospital, under the hammering pain of a disc hernia. That's when I remembered the Devil because pain is his thing. It isn't God's thing because if God spent his time making me suffer, he would be no better than a torturer. He wouldn't deserve my respect and, much less, my love...

I thought about Job. The sacred poems say that one nice day, God called together all his vassals. And among them was—know who?—him. Satan. The adversary. So a polite conversation started up between the two, God and Devil. After asking what he'd been up to, and being informed that he'd been walking all over earth, God asked him, "have you seen my servant Job? An extraordinary man, in him there are only good things. Job is a song of beauty. Ah! how I delight in hearing his music!"

"No wonder," the Devil replied. "You have surrounded him by only good things. It would be strange if he weren't singing, but let me put him to a test. Let me put him on my anvil and beat him with my hammer! Let's see if, after the superfluous has been pounded, when he is absolutely alone with your truth, if you still hear the same music..."

And I got the curious idea of the Devil being put in charge of the quality of the human being. He doesn't believe in appearances. He peels people like an onion, layer by layer, until he gets to the hidden interior, to see what's there. Will anything be there? Or will it be empty? I thought about this because it is precisely this that pain does: it takes away the layers, destroys the superfluous until the only thing left, there at the bottom, is the hour of truth.

That's why I stopped calling him The Tempter—a charged word of moral suggestion, as if his business were to trick people and throw them into Hell. I prefer to call him the Tester, the one makes us pass a test that submits us to quality control to see if inside that beautiful violin there isn't anything but moldy bread.

Other holy scriptures are more radical than that, suggesting that the Devil isn't a separate entity but is "the backside of God." The tester is God when he gets the anvil and the hammer That's what he did with Abraham, a good and happy man who never tired of playing on his flute the most beautiful praises of life, for the joy of a son, born beyond all expectations. And it is said that the moment came when God decided to make him pass a test. "Abraham, Abraham, take thy son, thy only son, whom you love, and offer him as a sacrifice on the mountain…" Let us see, Abraham, if without your son you continue to play your flute… Let see if you will be able to "contain death, the whole of death, gently, without becoming angry…" (Rilke) And the narration in the New Testament also says that it was the Spirit itself that drove Jesus into the desert (there where solitude is total, there where one says, "I am lost!", there where all shouts for help are useless, there where neither water nor bread exists, there where you hear the howl of death nearby…) to be tested by the Devil.

The truth that resides inside a person is known when the onion gets to the end and there are no more tricks of defense, no hole to hide in, no smiling mask, no deodorant to cover up the bad smell, no noise of parties or activity to distract us from our encounter with the abysm.

There, amid the pain, in the hospital, in Mephistophelean meditation, my tape player played a Beethoven sonata. And an affirmation came to me that not even my pain managed to silence: "Not even all the pain in the world would be able to alter this fact, that this sonata is infinitely beautiful, and it will be so for all eternity, even if there is no one left to hear it…"

So it was. I became thankful to the hammer and to the anvil for the thoughts they made me think.

The Terror of the Mirror

Everything indicates that eating a brick a day is bad for the health. Worse than two packs of cigarettes. However, I have never found a doctor who combatted this pernicious habit. They talk about the danger of fried hog fat, fatty steaks, fried foods, sugar, sedentary life, beer... But about the danger of ingesting bricks, the silence is total. Of course. There's no need. Nobody wants to eat bricks. The prohibition seems to be only where desire resides. Firemen are called when there's a fire. It is prohibited (uselessly) to covet the neighbor's wife (or husband).... Obviously, because coveting happens. It is also commanded that you honor your mother and father because, I imagine, even the Scriptures knew about Oedipus, the sinister mixture of hatred and prohibited desires that are mixed up with relationships between parents and children. And if it's prohibited to kill and steal, it's because these desires are quite alive within us. Prohibition reveals the presence of its counterpart, hidden on the reverse side.

All this is as introduction to the continuation of our demonological meditations, which have already begun. To absolve the Devil of an unfair accusation that's always made about him, that he puts impure thoughts in the heads of poor mortals. Nothing further from the truth. This power was not conceded to him. A desire cannot be put into the heart of anybody. What can be done is open the doors so that those which already exist, locked up and silenced, appear in the living where guests, in the grave company of clerics and moral principles, talk about things that they all agree with and which don't make anybody blush. The Devil doesn't throw trash in the well. He just messes around with the mud lying beneath the clean water. And then the toads, snakes, and scorpions start popping up—and the face of Narcissus turns ugly.

But that's not the thing the Devil's tricks make appear. The bottom of the waters is an enchanted place where beautiful creatures also live, mermaids, sea goddesses, butterflies with colorful wings, seagulls soaring through the air, sailboats coming to sea, and even a lovely sleeping woman. They live there, submerged, forgotten... But who submerged them? We ourselves. Some for being too ugly. They were chosen in shame, as long ago chamber pots were hidden in nightstands. Others, being just too beautiful, too daring, too free, we lacked the courage to take them as partners in fear of flying, in fear of sailing off, in fear of loving. Beauty extends invitations that frighten...

So that's all the Devil does: He awakens desires that already live within us. He doesn't lay the egg. He only breaks the egg that we lay—just to see what's inside, if it's life or death.

Subtle. Very subtle. The Scriptures say that the serpent was the most subtle of all the creatures God put in the Garden. It slides along with gentle talk to the place where our desires reside. I came to think that the serpent was the first psychoanalyst because both are looking for the same thing: forgotten desires.

That's where the second part of its task began. First it released desires. Then, as a subtle tester, it asks us a question: "Do you know that it isn't possible to keep all of them? You need to choose. If you had to reject all of them, save one, which would you choose? Where is your heart? What is your truth?" It begins like the way ophthalmologists put one lens after another to our eye and say, "this one or that one?" Which do you love more? What is your truth? And we go plucking petals off the flower to see which one's left, to see who we are. Because we are what we desire. The soul is a space where the most distinct songs play, wild rhythms of drums, cosmic Gregorian chants, heavy metal rock bands, sweet flutes, lullabies, love songs, military marches—all at the same time. And that makes us decide: "This one or that one?" In the end, which is yours?

And we come to a strange conclusion: The tester is at the service of love. It obliges us to decide. To the extent that we decide, the contortions in our face become clearer, reflected in the waters of the pool.

Álvaro de Campos has a verse that goes more or less like this: "I am the interval between my desire and that which others desire of me." Interval, an undefined space where my truth is lost in a spell cast by the requests of others. Others ask that we not be whom we are, that we be only what they wish. So we lose our face and have nothing but masks. Onions without a core, nothing but layers. The Devil puts us between the hammer and the anvil and forces us to make decisions. It could be that, in the end, we have the supreme experience of horror. When, in front of the mirror, we don't see any face at all, just the faces of others. I think that's why everyone talks bad about the Devil because, besides being a blacksmith with hammer and anvil, he is also a specialist in beauty with a mirror in his hand. and the reflection in the mirror hurts more than the hammer and anvil...

Autumn

Summer has finally gone, but not without some rudeness and tantrums: thunder, lightning, rain, floods. It didn't want to leave. I understand. It wanted to stay to see and court Autumn, which is much more beautiful than Summer. Summer, bummer: It refuses to accept the passage of time. It didn't want to say good-bye. It would have liked to stay. Life is so good! But time is implacable. The sun told Summer that the time of its departure had arrived. The sun was lower in the sky, its trips a little shorter each day, the nights a little longer, twilight arriving a little earlier, the mornings arriving a little later. Earlier, the wind invited you to take off your shirt. Now it causes gooseflesh and calls the sweaters from the drawers where they've been sleeping. The sky turns more blue. It must have been on an Autumn afternoon when the Beatles composed that ballad that goes "...because the sky is blue, it makes me cry...." And the green of plants becomes more deeper. In the Summer the excess of light obscured the colors. In the Autumn, light becomes more gentle and colors blossomed like flowers. Summer is restless. Everything about it invites you to go out and do something. Autumn is calm, introspective, inviting withdrawal and meditation. It's an invitation to thought.

I especially like Autumn's afternoons. Summer is the season of noon. Autumn is closer to sunset. And how the two are lovely, Autumn and afternoons. There's a hint of sadness in the air. Adélia Prado says, "The lovely fills the eyes with tears." The two are like each other because the two are full of good-byes.

The Afternoon

...it's this calmness of the sky
with its parallel clouds
and the last of the color penetrating the trees
even the birds.

It's this curve of the pigeons, skimming the rooftops,
this crowing of roosters and turtledoves, far away;
and, farther, the budding of white stars,
still without light...

In the city where I lived, in rural Minas Gerais, at twilight they played Ave Maria and it was as if all nature stopped and prayed. I liked to look at the trees. There was an absolute immobility in the air. Not a single tremor disturbed the thoughtful tranquility of the leaves. And the clouds at sunset were colored in light green, passing through the yellows, oranges, and reds, even purple, preparing to disappear into darkness. All beautiful. All sad. And we think thoughts different from those thought by day. For Wordsworth:

> *The clouds that gather round the setting sun*
> *Do take a sober colouring from an eye,*
> *That hath kept watch o'er man's mortality.*

Twilight and Autumn make us return to our truth. They say what we are. Metaphors of us ourselves, they make us remember that we are autumnal twilight beings. We are also beautiful and sad... Like late Summer, we, too, do not want to depart...Paul Bouget tells us:

> *When the rivers turn pink in the setting sun,*
> *and a warm breeze passes over the wheat fields,*
> *a command to be happy seems*
> *to emanate from all things*
> *And mounts towards the unquiet heart.*
> *A command to relish the charm of being alive*
> *while one is young and the evening is fine,*
> *for we are going as that stream goes:*
> *It to the sea - we to the tomb!*

Whoever stops to hear the voices of Autumn and the afternoon will notice that within their beauty they speak to us of our life and our death. Nothing morbid. Only those who learn the wisdom that death teaches can live well.

So it was that the professor of literature in the film *Dead Poets Society* began the learning of his students. Do you remember? He took them to a photograph where they found, frozen on paper, people. Now they were all dead. We, too, one day. The lesson of poetry is that you have to contemplate the twilight on the horizon to feel the incomparable beauty of the moment. There's no time for playing around. Carpe diem: harvest the day like something that will never repeat, like one who harvests the twilight "before breaking the silver chain and smashing the golden cup..." Drink each moment to the last drop. You need to look at the Abyss face to face to understand that Autumn has arrived and that afternoon is begun. Every moment is crepuscular. Every moment is autumnal. Its beauty announces its imminent dive into the horizon.

When the sun is at its zenith these ideas do not disturb us. Everything seems to be fine. There's still time. Work routines hide our truth. But they cannot impede the afternoon from arriving with its colors of good-bye, nor Autumn from arriving, announcing the nearness of winter. And they force us to have different thoughts, thoughts of loneliness. They are silent teachers. If we pay attention and listen to what they say, we will become wise. Because wisdom is this: to contemplate the Abyss without being destroyed by it. In the words of Rilke, "to contain death, the whole of death, gently, without becoming angry."

Revelation

Revelation happens suddenly, without warning. It's quite true that every day we look in the mirror. But this daily look is a look without perception.

For many years I knew my hair was falling. I noted that my bald spots were getting bigger. But I kept combing normally, without noticing that the part was always getting closer to the ear. It was a case of charming thinning hair. The mirror told me, but I didn't believe it. The moment of revelation happened in Recife at a series of improv comedians. One of them, to be nice, improvised a little poem, calling me "Doctor Bald." From that day on, I never again looked in the mirror the same way. I saw that it was useless to continue fighting with the part in my hair. But I didn't worry about it much, consoling myself with the memory of one of the greatest heroes of mythology, Ulysses (not the one in Brasilia, the one in the Odyssey...) was bald, too. And how Penelope loved him!

Sometimes the terrible revelation comes to us in the form of praise. "Wow, you're so well preserved!" Nobody who sees me every day is going to say something like that. Amazement at my surprising state of preservation can exist only in someone who hasn't seen me in a long time and who was hoping to find me in a more advanced state of deterioration. These experiences of astonishment and the elegies that reveal them happen, preferably, at family reunions, rare events that generally happen at burials, and class reunions commemorating 25 years since graduation. When I hear such a compliment, I always remember cucumbers preserved by the power of boiling, vinegar, and vacuum, and that, without the help of these tricks, they would have rotted long ago. It's as if the praise included a question about the physio-chemical trick that made the farce of my preserved appearance. Was it plastic surgery or macrobiotic diet? But, looking around, we understand that we can't be much different from others.

But none of these revelations has ever impressed me until I took that punch in the head. This happened a few years ago. I was feeling good and happy in São Paulo. I took the subway. The car was full. Which doesn't bother me in the least. I leaned up against one of those vertical pipes and went into one of my favorite pastimes: observing people's faces. Faces suggest many stories. And so I went, from face to face until my eyes met eyes that were observing me. Surely that person had a pastime similar to mine: trying to guess the stories that reside in me. She was a young woman of calm physiognomy and almost smiling. Her eyes did not deviate from mine, and for a moment I felt happy. That was when I took the punch. Her almost-smile turned into a smile, her eyes looking into mine: She got up and offered me her seat.

Her gesture allowed no argument. Her terrible kindness (she couldn't imagine how terrible her kindness was!) obliged me. I sat down. I no longer looked into her eyes so that she wouldn't perceive my shock. I knew that she had liked me. If not, she wouldn't have looked at me in that gentle way and would not have offered me a place. It's just that she liked me in an unexpected way, liked me in a way I didn't want to be liked. I saw, reflected in her eyes, an image of mine that I had never seen. Maybe I looked like her father (whether alive or dead I cannot know). Or maybe I just represented another age, worthy of special deference on the part of those younger. In the end, old age is the age when it gets hard to sustain the weight of your own body on your own legs. She, young, could stay on her feet; I old, deserved to be seated. Her terrible kindness had set me far away, very far from her, in a world apart.

It would have been much easier to confront a rudeness. If she hadn't made the kind gesture, I would have remained in the illusion and carried within myself that moment of happiness. But she wasn't good at guessing the secrets of the soul. She made the gesture, I took the punch, and the revelation occurred. I saw myself, in the honest mirror of her eyes, old.

But don't go thinking that getting old is bad. It has its advantages. A friend of mine told me, in the middle of laughter, that he was preparing a list of projects that he was shelving as a result of old age. He was giving up jumping from Gálvea Rock by delta-wing. He no longer thought about skiing down the Alps. He wasn't expecting to see his name among the players invited to join the Brazilian volleyball team. And above all, he was no longer making plans for amorous affairs with Bruna Lombardi.

To get old is to give up reaching for the high stars in the distant future. Now it is time for happiness. Each new day is a miracle of grace, a cup of pleasure that ought to be drunk to the end, without leaving anything for tomorrow. Tempus fugit! Therefore, carpe diem—seize the day that begins as one picks a flower that will never happen again.

Let's go, don't cry!
Infancy is lost,
childhood is lost,
The first love has passed,
The second love has passed,
The third love has passed.
But the heart continues.
You've lost your best friend,
You haven't attempted any journey.
You don't own a house, boat, or land.
You don't have a dog...

What image could be more true to happiness? A dog is a comfort—you can be sure of that—that will never abandon you. It's a metaphor of unconditional love, of the look that always forgives, of the presence that's always there. To understand this, I think, is to be a little wiser.

Retired

As hard as I looked, I was able to find only one: that of Quincas Berro d'Água. The deeds of retired men aren't good for literature. They lack the ingredients that give flavor to an active narrative. They no longer perform athletic feats, they're out of the fight for power, and they aren't the type ideal for big, amorous adventures. Quinca sBerro d'Água was an exception. A quiet man with habits like those of a wagon ox, used to pulling a load without complaint, obedient to the switch, that's how the silent Quincas was, a loyal public servant who at the end of the month handed his whole salary over to his wife, with a fine, dry voice, a characteristic he passed on to this daughter, his faithful ally.

That's how Quincas lived, pondering his immense loneliness. It would never go through anyone's mind that inside that man, ready for retirement, there lived young dreams of freedom and love. The revelation happened on the day when he completed his last days for retirement. Quincas returned home just as always, silent, dragging along, doing nothing to raise suspicions of what would happen in a few moments. He went to his bedroom. His wife and daughter thought he was going to put on his pajamas and slippers, the only uniform appropriate for someone who has retired. But a few moments later, Quincas came out, a little suitcase in his hand. The burning voice of his wife pierced his ears with "Where do you think you're going?" It was followed by the serpentine rattle of his daughter. Quincas did not respond. From inside him came a savage scream that they had never imagined: Vipers! And with no further explanation, he disappeared out the door. And thus begins the story of a happy retiree... Anyone who wants to know the rest can read the text by Jorge Amado.

I remembered a long story of a retiree. A theater piece I saw, many years ago, the name of which I have forgotten. The scene took place in a bank. Could there be a more disagreeable place to spend a life? Numbers, numbers, numbers...only numbers. But the air was of a party. One of the employees, already bald and using dentures, was retiring. Everyone was talking about it. The end of the suffering was finally arriving for one of them. From then on he would be free, totally free, to do what he wanted. No more clocking in, no more checks, duplicates, promissory notes, accounts that had to add up. He could sleep when he wanted, do what he felt like doing. The desire that for 35 years had been trapped inside the cage was going to fly through space without end. The others smiled with envy and counted the days remaining until their own wonderful day.

The second act happened after his retirement. So do you know what he went on to do after retirement? Every day, without fail, he went to the bank and stayed there, with no desk to sit at, without anything to do, watching, watching, with longing and sadness in his eyes…. The poor guy! He had spent so many years in the cage that he had forgotten how to fly. He didn't know what to do with the infinite.

It isn't by chance that often retirees soon die. A friend of mine, whom I met at the market (one of my favorite pastimes. It's good to see the stands of vegetables, the fruits, the flowers, the fish…), knowing that I was going to retire, warned me: "Look, don't go and die…" I trembled before this prophetic warning, but I calmed myself, thinking that this wasn't going to happen to me. I calmed myself, *pero no mucho…*

I started thinking about this strange thing, that it's exactly the liberation to do what you want that is the beginning of death. The situation is worse for men than for women, I think. Our social arrangements decree that the house belongs to the woman. I remember, back in Minas, that holidays were the terror of the *donas de casa*, the housewives. (I've never heard this expression applied to a husband, *dono de casa*, the househusband.) The husbands hang around like condemned souls, walking around the house, ducking into the kitchen, giving advice. Until they are expelled from the place where they don't belong, with an affirmation with which they concur: "A man's place is in the street!" And there they go, out to the public square without knowing what to do.

It's a division of space that surely comes from the time when men were hunters. Their place was in the infinite world. A domestic man is the man who has lost the dignity of the hunter. Feminists, with all good reason, rebel against the word domestic to describe the profession of women who don't want to venture forth on a hunt. Now a more delicate word is used: dona do lar—the home woman. But it's the same thing. What it's saying is that the house is hers. Have you ever imagined the same expression being used to describe the status of a retired man?

Poor retiree…He's without place. I think that's why before long he dies. At home, he doesn't know what to do. He never learned to inhabit that space. He lacks authority and savoir-faire. To do anything, he has to ask permission. If, by chance, he decides to visit his old place of employment, his apparition causes the fright of a soul from another world. A few days ago, a professor at the University of São Paulo at Campinas (Unicamp) asked me: "What are you doing here? Are you lost?" And I understood there was neither weeping nor candles: things continued as normal, without me there.

I therefore advise all who are going to retire, that they lose their fantasies of retirement being the beginning of a time of happiness. It could even be… But for that, the caged bird must remember how to fly. And if you asked me how a caged bird can remember how to fly, my answer would be simple: it has to remember how to dream. One who is rich in dreams never grows old. He or she might all of a sudden die. But the death would be mid-flight. Which is quite lovely.

Candles

*C*hristmas is coming. I'm scared. Scared of the insanity. Christmas is a time when people get all bothered. They sing *Silent Night*. But their bodies and souls are at war, possessed by agitation and rush. When Baby Jesus was born, the Devil ran away. I make use of candles to exorcise insanity. For a whole year I have left them forgotten in the dark of a cabinet. A puff of my breath put them to sleep. And asleep they have stayed, like Sleeping Beauty, waiting for the flame that would awaken them. They look dead. But I know that a touch of fire will bring them to life again. They await resurrection. How human they are! They look like us. Our hardened bodies, too, can burn again. All they need is to be touched by the magic of fire!

I need them, my candles. Their faithful flames calm me. "Do you want to become calm?" old Gaston Bachelard asked. "Breathe softly before the delicate candle as it calmly performs the work of illumination."

So different from lamps! Would it be possible, perchance, to love a lamp? What tame emotions might be born of its strong and indifferent light? Who would call those emotions up from my lamp? All lamps are the same. When they burn out, they inspire no sadness, only the inconvenience of exchanging them for others.

Candles are different. They cry while they illuminate. Their tears, born of fire, spill over and run down their body. They cry because they know that, to shine, they must die. It's impossible to contemplate a candle in its work of illumination without feeling a little sad. Its flame, modest, softened by indecision and tremors, makes me reflect back on myself. I'm the same. My flame vacillates when touched by the wind. That's why I can call the candle mine. We are made of the same substance. We have a fate in common. Candles tell different stories. Each one has a name that is its alone. One of them I stuck in the mouth of an empty wine bottle. Its colored tears ran down the glass and hardened. No handkerchief will dry them up. They stay there like memories of past moments that took place within its light and intimacy. Presences of an absence, lost time crystallized... My attentive gaze passes over their wrinkles. I note that there are various colors. That wine bottle has already held several candles. Green, red, and yellow tears mix and cover each other in a fabric of wax—generations that consumed themselves in the same fate of gently glowing. I look for the candle that ought to be there to be awakened. I see that she no longer exists. She was consumed, consumed until her last bit melted. She didn't spill a single tear. She simply fell into the bottle and disappeared. I see the female form of the bottle. It's a uterus with its vaginal opening pointed high, like the steeple of a cathedral.

I thought that maybe the candle was telling me that dying is like a disinclination to be born, a return to the maternal womb. I was touched because, in fact, a light that lit in moments past stopped lighting. It had sunk into the bottle. That candle would never again be lit. All that's left is the memory of its moments of light. I think about what I should do. Leave the bottle as it is, with its colorful tears and emptiness? Or put another candle in there? No, the beauty of that bottle is due to precisely the testimony of successive generations that left their lives engraved on the glass. The flame must continue to shine. When a candle finishes, another must take its place.

A different candle is ashamed to cry. It hides inside a metal cup that doesn't let its tears overflow. It cries quietly, without flaunting. Blocked from overflowing, its tears turn into a flat and luminous interior lake of melted wax where the flame is reflected. Weeping has that power. It can make light more luminous. The candle refuses to let go of its pain. It holds back its tears, keeps them tight to its body, embracing them, recognizing them as part of itself. That's what poets do. Their light is modest, hidden in metal, hiding from the eye. But their flesh of wax is full of the delicious fragrance of cinnamon. When she cries, the air fills with beauty. I think perhaps this candle was made for those who can't see. Her perfumed light calms even those who have their eyes closed.

I take another candle into my hands. It's almost as thick as the bottle. In its ochre wax an artist has engraved leaves and flowers in relief. Even unlit it's beautiful. Sensitive hands that touch it can feel the drawings. The weak flame melted its own body, drank its own flesh. The flame shines from inside the vessel that the flame opened. The sculpted skin, too far from the heat, survived intact. Contemplated from afar, it gives the impression of solidity and permanence. But all you have to do is light the flame to see its fragility. The more worn by its fire, the more its skin became translucent and the light is filtered through its ephemeral flesh. What a magnificent lesson for candles—only the bodies worn out by the fire of love can become transparent!

Love prefers the light of candles. Maybe because that's everything we wish for a beloved—that she or he be a soft light that helps us tolerate the terror of the night. Under the light of love that gently and patiently shines, the dark no long scares us so. It's a silent night!

Don't let your candles go out! Darkness is lonely and sad! Touch them again with the flame of love!

Time to Die

$\mathcal{J}$have many fears. But I'd never thought about that one, the biggest of them all. But all it took was for the reporter to present a question for the fear to appear, terrible and clear, before me. "What is it that you fear the most?" And all of a sudden, I saw the scene: a body with half-closed eyes that see nothing, mechanical respiration, tubes into nostrils and mouth, heart beating to electric stimulation, the beeps on the monitors telling of a life that maintained in that body where once there had been Life but now knew nothing of what was happening around it... And I responded with a certainty I rarely have: "What I fear most is that they would oblige me to live when my body only wishes to die...."

They have given the term "heroic measures" to the technological paraphernalia that is used to keep alive a body that wishes to die... But the hero is someone robust with vitality, with bright eyes, body pulsing with desire and with a will for gallant action. What similarity with a hero

127

is there in "heroic measures"? None. It would be better if the term were "desperate measures." Who is the hero? Certainly not the person who just wants to leave. They decree that with these wonders of science, life triumphs over death. To me it seems the opposite, that it's death triumphing over life.

For what is life? It seems we no longer know. Do we still know what living is? Maybe that's why, having forgotten how to live, we have lost the wisdom of knowing how to die. I remember some lines from Eliot:

> *All our knowledge brings us nearer to our ignorance,*
> *All our ignorance brings us nearer to death,*
> *But nearness to death no nearer to God.*
> *Where is the Life we have lost in living?*
> *Where is the wisdom we have lost in knowledge?*

Having lost the wisdom of living, we don't dare answer, so we ask machines to answer for us.

I thought about Human Rights and asked myself whether some provision has been made to protect the right to die with dignity. Because to die with dignity should be a right guaranteed for all who live. Death is part of life, the last act, and it is undignified that this right be taken from anyone...

"Reverence for life": With these words Albert Schweitzer summarized the essence of his philosophy, learned in the mystery of African nights, where all of nature pulsed like a live heart, from the most infinitesimal insect to the secrets of the jungle to the largest of animals.

Nothing more sacred exists. Nothing can be the object of greater reverence.

But, what is life? Life is eyes that greet the dawn, caress the nights, welcome smiles; ears that take in the sound of wind, hear groans of pain, listen to words of love; mouths that try the delights of fruit and kisses and which recite poems; noses that smell low tide, food in the oven and on sweaty bodies. Legs that walk through the woods and carry messages to distant places, arms that plant gardens and reach out for hugs and struggles. Life is an enormous poem, an explosion of acts and feelings spread across space. But like all things human, life is also weariness that longs for sleep. As the holy poet says, "for everything under the sun there is a season; a time to be born and a time to die." To know how to live is to know how to die. Every poem leans toward its final word; every song extends to its silence. The last word in which reverberates all those that came before: silence where echo all the sounds that prepared it. All life is a preparatio mortis. That's why the lst word and the last act are a right that no one can steal from you. To the body belongs the right to say: "It's time to leave." That's why Manuel Bandeira declared that his last act ought to be a poem. Because that was what his life was full of.

Here's how I want my last poem:
That it be loving, saying the simplest and least intentional things

That it be ardent like a sigh without tears
That it have the beauty of flowers nearly without
aroma
The purity of the flame that consumes the clearest
diamonds
The passion of suicides who kill themselves without
explanations.

Mothers know when children ask to go to sleep even without saying a single word. Mothers know the silent language of their children's bodies. And when this moment comes, the only act of love is to take them into their lap and let them sleep, without fear. Life is a child. It plays in the morning, works until midday, loves in the afternoon. But it comes to the time of twilight, the time of weariness… Ah! What a terrible thing to not be able to rest! Fernando Pessoa suffered to think about the unrelenting weariness of the stars…

I feel sorry for the stars
Which have shined so long,
So long, so long…
I feel sorry for the stars.
Isn't there a weariness
Felt by things,
By all things,
A weariness of existing,
Of being,
Just of being,
Whether shining sad or smiling…
Is there not, finally,

130

For all things that are,
Not death, but yes,
Some other finality?
Or a higher purpose,
or something like that,
Some kind of pardon?

It isn't the stars but we who in that way need a higher purpose...such as a poem or a song. And who in this world has the right to rob anyone of the right to say, "It is time to leave..."?

But for that—to not be destroyed by feelings of guilt for agreeing with the body's request that asks to leave—we need to know how to listen the silent request of children who want to sleep. But who still has this wisdom? For a long time medicine has not heard what the body says. It is no longer able to decipher the enigmatic messages of the face. The truth is, it isn't even necessary to look at the eyes. Look at the exams, examine the charts, palpate the organs: biochemical messages, electric revelations, transparencies of the insides...it knows the language of machines: A long time ago it forgot the language of the face, the eyes, the voice..."Doctor, I am afraid..." Then ideas get mixed up. Nothing has been learned about this. (Among those who struggle against death, isn't there a terrible fear of hearing its voice?) And anyway, it's irrelevant... To those who struggle against death, nothing is taught about the wisdom of listening to life and talking about its last wish, to leave...

No, no I don't want heroic measures. I only want pain

not to torture me so I can hear a last poem, hear a last sonata. Only in this way will the *adeus* be something sweet, a manifestation of life at its last moment, and the emptiness that follows will fill with the sweet nostalgia named longing...We need to re-learn the sacred wisdom: If there is a time to be born, there is also a time to die. May the last moment be as beautiful as a sunset, far from the cold electric-metal of machines...

The Doctor

...*A*nd all of a sudden, a corner of my memory that forgetfulness had hidden lights up, and I see again, the same way I saw it the first time: the painting. I see myself, a boy, in waiting a room of a medical practice. I was sick. My frightened eyes looked over the things around me. Until they found it. It was hanging, along on the white wall. I got up and went over to see it better. I read the title of the painting: *The Doctor*.

It's the living room of a house. Familiar scene.

Everything is sunk in shadow except the central place, lit by the light of a lamp. But the light is useless. The most lighted place is the darkest: a sick girl. The clarity of the details is only enough to indicate the place where the mystery is deeper. When the light comes on above the abyss, the abyss becomes darker. Her eyes are shut, sunk in a febrile forgetfulness. She knows nothing that goes on around her. Where is she going? Infinitely far, in an unknown place, where nothing can touch her. Her arm hang inert over the emptiness.

The lamp illuminates the sick girl. But the eyes of anyone examining the painting with attention don't trust it, and they notice the presence of another light. From the kerosene lamp comes a light that illuminates the girl. But from the sick girl comes a light that illuminates the whole scene: a sad light, a somber light that floods the room with its mystery: the light of death. Death, too, has its light.

The artist chose things intentionally. If, instead of a girl it were an old man, death would have been something different. Death has many faces. The death of the old, painful though it may be, is part of the natural order of things. After the twilight comes the night. The death of the elderly is sad, but it isn't tragic. It's like the final chord of a sonata. The end is what it was supposed to be. But the death of one's child is a mutilation.

The light of life is happy, playful, a riot of color, it lives with such exuberance that it can give itself the luxury of squander. Everything large and small, important or not, becomes colorful at its touch. The light of death, however, only illuminates the essential. In that living room you know the essential truth. The whole universe is pulled in. In the absolute center around which all worlds turn, there is a sick little girl. What are mountains and seas worth, men, their business, their loves and wars, if in that room a little girl struggles with death?

The Doctor

In a corner, the mother and father, are images of powerlessness. They don't know what to do and can't do anything. The mother is collapsed on a table. Her face is sunken in emptiness. The only thing she can do is cry. Her husband, standing, rests a hand on his wife's shoulder. But I imagine that she doesn't feel anything. At that moment she isn't a wife or even a housewife. She's a mother, just a mother. Her husband's gesture, what does it mean to say? Might it be an attempt at consolation, as if to say, "I am here"? Poor consolation! Or is it the opposite, a discreet search for support, as if to say, "I, too, am helpless." It's all a departure ready to happen. And love, the most joyous thing, is shown as the saddest thing. In the face of death, love takes on tragic colors.

The father is dressed in a heavy cloak. It's strange! Why so much clothes inside the house? The cloak tells us of a trip through the cold, helplessness in search of help. Doctor, come quick! My daughter... He returned and didn't remember to take it off. What matters the discomfort of a cloak inside the house when your daughter struggles with death?

Beside the girl sits a stranger: the doctor. For isn't the doctor a stranger? Yes, a stranger because he doesn't belong in the daily life of the family. Nevertheless, when there's a struggle between love and death, he's the one who's called.

The doctor thinks hard. His elbow is resting on his knee. His chin is rest in his hand. He isn't thinking about what to do. The potions on the little table show that what can be done has been done. His meditative form occurs after carrying out the medical measures, after depleting his knowledge and his power. It would be good if he could withdraw, for he has already done what he can do... But no. He remains. He waits. He has to live with his powerlessness. Maybe he's praying. Everyone prays when love finds itself powerless. Prayer is this: this communion with love above the emptiness... Maybe he is silently asking forgiveness from the parents for being so weak in the face of death. And maybe his meditative waiting is a confession. I, too, am suffering...

I loved this painting the first time I saw it, without understanding it. Maybe it's the reason why, when I was a young man, for many years I dreamed of being a doctor. I loved the beauty of the image of a solitary man in struggle against death. In the face of death, we are all alone. We love the doctor not for his knowledge, not for his power, but for the human solidarity shown in his meditative waiting. And all his failures (for aren't they all condemned to lose the last battle?) will be forgiven if, in our helplessness, we see that he, silently, remains and ponders along with us.

Today you don't see this painting in the waiting rooms of doctors' offices. Modernity has transferred death from the home, the place of love, to institutions, places of power.

And doctors have been pulled from this scene of intimacy and put into another, where the wonders of technology turn insignificant the powerless pondering before death.

The Doctor

But the beautiful scene has not disappeared. It survives in many as memory and nostalgia, in the nooks of institutions. To these doctors, whose name need not be said (they know who they are), who silently ponder before the mysterious abyss of human tragedy, I offer my own powerless pondering. I look at them with the same eyes as the boy who for the first time confronted the beauty of this scene in the waiting room of a doctor's office.

Envy

I'm reading the poem by Ricardo Reis. The words run like the waters of a river. Everything about them is tranquility. They speak of the happiness that is possible in us:

Come sit with me, Lydia, by the river's edge.
Quietly watch it flow and learn
That life goes on, and our hands aren't clasped.
(Let's clasp hands.)
Let's love without fuss,
Let's pick flowers.
You gather them and leave them
In your lap, and let their scent soften the moment...

I have the habit of marking the margins of pages to help me remember where to find words that have made me think. But my pencil didn't make any mark beside these beautiful things that the poet wrote. It only left a sign of itself to the side of strange lines of dubious meaning that warn about the "big uneasiness" that disturbs the calmness of the two lovers at the river's edge. It's the line that speaks of "envies, which produce too much movement of the eyes."

I know that agitated eyes reveal a disturbed heart. When the heart is calm, the eyes also become calm. But I didn't know that envy has the power to agitate eyes.

That envy is an illness of the eyes. The word itself says so. It is derived from the Latin, in-videre, which means, literally, "to askew," a "twisted look," as opposed to a frank look with nothing to hide. Something bad resides in the envious eye, something scary with the power to destroy everything about the face, the evil eye: plants wilt, animals die, people get sick. That's why they have invented all kinds of defenses against envious eyes: horned cow skulls, prayers, magic acts, sprigs of rue, baths of aromatic herbs, incense with special aromas, spiritual passages.

If you believe in that, the poet's assertion that "envies produce too much movement in the eyes" becomes even more mysterious because the evil and envious look isn't a look of much movement. It has a fixed look, wanting to penetrate deeply. It lingers over the subject like a horsefly that lays its eggs in a wound.

It was a story they told me that revealed that the poet is right. It's about a man who found a bottle where a genie lived. It had the power to make dreams come true. Told a different way, it is about a man who found heaven—because heaven is just that, the place where our dreams come true. The genie came out of the bottle where he'd been sleeping and said to the man, "I have the power to make all your dreams come true, without limit. All you have to do is tell me your dream, and it shall happen."

The man then began to think about the wonderful things he might ask for: a young body without pain or illness, full of beauty, energy, houses in the most beautiful places in the mountains or on beaches, with gardens more lovely than those of the House of Dinda; wineries of the most fine wines, kitchens where the most delicious food is made, music, books, friends, love... Ah! He was a wise and refined man and knew about the things that make humans happy. And so his eyes went calmly walking through his dreams, enjoying beforehand the unlimited happiness that he would experience in a few moments.

That's when the genie said: "There's just one detail I forgot to mention because I think it's irrelevant. Everything you get, your worst enemy will get double..." Just as the genie said it, what happened to the man's eyes was just as the poet had said. The eyes that had until then rested on things that made him happy beyond his imagining began to looks at the things his enemy was going to have. And when he went back to his own stuff, the same stuff which just a moment before had made him the happiest man in the world, it had gone rotten. Comparison is a worm that makes delicious fruit rot. Envy leaves us with empty hands. It's important to understand this so you can understand the end of the story.

"I know what I want to ask for," the man said to the

genie after long thought.

"Then make your request," the genie said.

"Take out one of my eyes."

$\mathcal{AIDS}$

They've asked me to say something about AIDS in the language of poetry. It seems difficult, but it's not. Knowing how to look at things is enough. We look, wait, and all of a sudden, the thing becomes transparent. We begin to see things that aren't there. My artist friend looked at a cow pie and a mobile of luminous golden circles. Neruda looked at a common onion and his eyes saw crystal scales on a water rose.... We give this practice the name "dream." Poetic talk is the language of dreams. I said the terrible word and what I saw was frightened eyes "without recourse and fixed on a nearby horizon."... I then thought that to talk about AIDS is to talk about the terror of death approaching. But before long my dream changed and I saw other eyes in which the same horizon appeared. But it had a crepuscular beauty. Then I thought that death, always terrible, can be beautiful.

143

A friend I had, Alexander Schmemann, a poet theologian, discovered that in his brain there was an inoperable tumor. He understood that his time to leave was nigh. So he said to his wife, "The moment has arrived to celebrate the evening liturgies." And from that moment on, until the end, he dedicated himself to things he judged essential: music, pottery, the contemplation of nature, peaceful conversation with a few friends invited over for a glass of wine. Someone else I knew, who recognized that leukemia gave him just a year of life and that there was no more time to put things off, bought a little country place he'd always dreamed of and lived with his wife in as much love as he had never loved her before.

Milan Kundera says that we begin to love a woman at the moment we associate her face with a poetic metaphor. The same thing can be done with regard to death. And this is the meaning of all sacred words of religion: an enormous effort to clothe the terrible with the beauty of poetry. And that which is going to die therefore appears with the beauty of the lone sailor who gets into his little boat at the infinite sea. Or like the hiker who goes along up paths that take him to the tops of mountains covered in fog. Or like the one who leaves luminous trails where everyone walks and accepts the dark forest's invitation to the mysterious.

Death has two sides. One is its physical reality. In this they are all the same. The other side is the words we tell each other in the face of it. That's where we find the difference.

AIDS makes everyone speak in whispers—as if they were in the face of the shameful terrible. Long and winding though their trails may be, they all know where it comes from: It is born of two lovers in the embrace of a cursed and prohibited love. A secret place, it should be forever shut, like a prohibited room. We all have a secret room where no one may enter. There lives our deepest intimacy, which no eyes should see. That's why we cover ourselves with clothes, to protect our nakedness from the cruel eyes of strangers.

But death breaks down the door and turns the intimacy into a museum room open to the public. And when this happens, that which was lived, like passion, turns into pornography. Pornography isn't in the embrace but in the many eyes that watch it like a show.

So AIDS has two pains: the pain of the infirmity and the pain of the eyes of others. Its death, then is clothed in the words of shame, curse words that should be said in a whisper. And even the religions call it divine punishment for the cursed love.

Later, it's the pain of loneliness. Born of the intimacy of prohibited love, its revelation making any intimacy prohibited, the AIDS patient lives inside the aseptic bubble of a hospital. Not for his or her protection. The patient doesn't need to be protected. It's others who must be protected from the patient's love because it's lethal. And all around his body, the threads and webs go silently wrapping around his body, a terrible poem that turns into a cage and which says, 'Abandon all hope of love, you who enter here..." And closeness, any contact, any care, any hug is always prohibited.

Sometimes the idea comes to me that we are all contaminated with AIDS. Because in all of our bodies death does its silent work in our bodies. Blood tests don't show anything, but the mirror tells the truth...

What differentiates us isn't that some of us are healthy, others ill. We are all infected with the same illness. For that reason we are all brothers and sisters. The difference is in the poems that we recite before the horizon that approaches. And it's with these words that life resists in its battle against death. Because the body, as the scriptures say, isn't fed with bread alone—or medicines—but with every word that issues from the mouth of God. The language of God is poetry. And it is beauty that awakens in us the desire to live.

Who knows: there may be poets who know how to give AIDS patients the words that will pull them from the graves where our eyes have put them. And then we will eat of the same food...

The Shadow

So, I got sick—something sudden and scary—and while the doctors at the hospital turned me inside out to see what was happening with my body, I had to get along alone to deal with the turbulence that the matter was stirring up in my soul.

Really alone, the presence of other people unimportant to me, dear though they might be. Every sick person is immediately alone, inside a clear and impenetrable bubble. And it doesn't help to hold his or her hand. Not even loving care has the key to enter this solitude. It's the solitude of death. That's what makes sickness, even the most banal (because you never know for sure…). It obliges us to think about the possibility of death.

That's the reason conversation around the sickbed always bears the mark of dissemblance. Everyone feels the presence of the Shadow, but they do everything to ignore it. I remember these lines from T.S. Eliot, and I thought that they might be recited after a visit to a patient in the hospital:

> *Who is the third who walks always beside you?*
> *When I count, there are only you and I together*
> *But when I look ahead up the white road*
> *There is always another one walking beside you*
> *Gliding wrapt in a brown mantle, hooded*
> *I do not know whether a man or a woman*
> *—But who is that on the other side of you?*

No, don't think that they are only morbid thoughts. The dialogue with death provokes unexpected associations of humor. I confess, for example, that when I'm submitted to those horrible and humiliating examinations, I had a special love of the Pope. Not that, in extremis, I had converted and gone to find comfort in his monotone sermons pronounced in a clerical voice. What happened was that at one of those moments, an idea suddenly came to me: "Do this to the Pope, too..." And I started to laugh. Separated by my mind and by teachings, illness unites us with strange sacraments! I concluded that at least we have one thing in common... In the eventuality of our meeting in the future, we will have a lot to say about scatology, if not within the context of the the latest in science technology, then at least in the second meaning that ambiguity preserves and the Aurélio dictionary clarifies...

It's hard to understand that the inevitable dialogue with death which illness obliges us to have can also bring joys. Because that's just what happened.

I don't know if you have ever noticed that people find it much easier to express their hatreds and angers than their penchants and affections. I've asked many times about the reasons for this absurd moral defect, and the only explanation that comes to mind is that by letting hatred and anger explode, people feel like tigers, powerful, terrible predators. While when they show their penchants, they feel like defenseless birds, totally ridiculous, prisoners in the other person's cage. And to not feel imprisoned, they prefer to leave their penchants imprisoned in silence...

But when we get sick, the situation changes. No one fears sick people. They are imprisoned in their own invisible and impenetrable bubble. So there's no danger in their saying how they feel...

A lot of people phoned me. People I don't know, never saw and quite likely will never see. If I were a politician or a candidate for something, I would think they were seedlings to harvest when ripe. Poor politicians! They can never believe in the pure friendship that never expects to get anything back. But since I am like that tree that isn't good for anything and which the timber cutters leave high on the mountain, I have been given the grace of believing what they tell me. I know that they tell me what they tell me without hope of getting anything back. They only want to sit in my shade.

Because that's all they know about me: my shade...   *149*
And maybe that's why they love me: because they only

know my shadow. My shadow isn't me. It's these things I write. One of these anonymous people who called me on the phone, a woman of 70 years, said, "I don't want to die. Life is good!" I think she summarized, with these words, this shade in which we sit and which unites us in an invisible web of friendship. Together we share the pleasure of living! In each one of us lives a Zorba who, at the moment of death, grabs hold of the window, looks to the horizon that opens outside, and shouts, "A man like me has to live a thousand years!"

Come Visit Me

The day dawned bright. At my window the first blue morning glory opened, the flower that Walt Whitman said brought him more happiness than all the books of philosophy combined. I looked to the blue sky like my own little flower. A few clouds, anchored in that sea of tranquility. Clouds always make me dream. Since I was a boy I have liked to lie in the grass and look up at them, imagining they were animals, ships, profiles of fantastical beings, trees in celestial forests. I looked at one of them and had the impression it was you—a motorcyclist who flew down the trails of the endless mystery.

When my mother died—an elderly woman of 93—my brother told me that she suffered imagining her body, so fragile and unprotected, walking among cold and empty space... The death of someone does that. We start asking: "Where will I wander?" I must admit that I think it's bad taste and lack of imagination, the custom of visiting the graves of the dead. Some believe this is proof of love. I think the opposite. Because it's as if we imagine that they are there, in an eternal shroud of earth and stone. I would rather imagine that they are wandering in other places.

Where do you wander? Cecília Meireles asked the same question in the face of her grandmother's death: "Where will your body be? In the wall? In the furniture? In the ceiling?" But these limits, if they had been able to gather up that body while alive, were too small for it after death. Su cadáver estaba lleno de mundo, said Vallejo in a masterful verse. Your other body now sails together with the white clouds, following the design of flying doves, wandering through the orchards laden with fruit, sitting on the beach before a shimmering sea...

I don't understand anything about the other world. But I don't approve of what I hear from specialists in the subject. They say that there, everyone becomes serious, speaking of important things, walking in a paced and solemn manner, like ethereal creatures. I think it's different. People go back to being children, without hearing their mother's voice saying, "Be careful you don't fall!" "Don't get your clothes dirty!" "It's time to sleep!" In the other world, it's the children who give orders. This isn't something I made up. It's there in the Gospel, from the mouth of the divine son of God, who said that to go to heaven is the same as becoming a child again. Which provoked the fear of the serious Nicodemus, who understood everything by the letter of the law, without the soul of a poet. He imagined that old people would have to once again enter the womb of their mother. He didn't know that the child never dies. She lives within us forever, locked in, and from inside the idiocy of adulthood she must be born... God is a child. Alberto Carneiro knew this. he said, "The Eternal Child is the God that was missing, the human that is natural, the divine that smiles and plays. That's how we go down the road, jumping and singing and laughing and enjoying our common secret, which is to know, everywhere, that there is no mystery in the world and that everything is worthwhile..."

You've already been a sexagenarian. You've had a friend who's a sexagenarian, and his or her terror wasn't age. It was fear of getting run over and being reported in the newspaper "Sexagenarian run over!" Have you ever imagined how terrible it would have been if in your obituary it said, "Sexagenarian died in a motorcycle accident"? Nobody would have been surprised since they all knew you were a child.

Where will you wander? I know you must be wandering wherever you always wanted to go: by motorcycle, over the trails of the Mantiqueira Range, looking at distant horizons and nearby creeks.... the child always returns to the places where the joy of play resides. And that's the beautiful earth we play with.

I went to my bookshelf and found the famous letter of an Indian chief, addressed to the president of the United States. The whites wanted to buy some land from them. He was horrified with the idea since, for them, the Indians,

153

land was the eternal part of the soul. "The dead of the white men forget their land of origin when they go walk among the stars. Our dead never forget this lovely earth because she is the mother of the red man. We are part of the earth, and she is part of us. The perfumed flowers are our sisters, the hart, the horse, and the great eagle are our brothers. The rocky peaks, the humid furrows of the fields, the warm body of the foal, and man—they all belong to the same family."

I don't think you're going to walk among the stars. They're too far, too solitary, too hot... You will prefer the same trails through the woods, the same creeks, the same pines...

Death is very strange. She's the owner of an insuperable wisdom. For me she has been a teacher of life. I learn a lot from her. But when she stops being a teacher of wisdom and goes on to do stuff, it disrupts everything. If she had asked for my advice, you would still be alive. I would have passed into her hands a long list of priorities that I have prepared, people who, if they went to the other world, this one would be better off. Everybody has a little list like that... But Death never asks anyone's advice. And so you went, when you should have stayed.

I, too, love the same places that you loved. I even have a little place. I don't need to give you a map since you already know everything. Appear. I won't be afraid. What I'm really afraid of is to find myself among the living that death has forgotten...

On Laughter and Joy

Because, in case you don't know it,
this is what life is made of, only moments.
Don't lose the now.
Jorge Luis Borges

"Carpe diem!"

We have felt very little joy.
That, only that, is our original sin.
Nietzsche

Joy

Shortly before dying, Roland Barthes held his inaugural conference as a professor at the College de France. He knew he was getting old, but he welcomed it as a time of starting over, the beginning of a vita nuova. And to end his talk he made an astounding personal confession. He said that the time had come to turn himself over to the forgetting of everything he had learned. Time to unlearn. Snakes, to continue living, have to abandon their old skin. He also had to abandon the body of knowledge with which tradition had involved him. Only in this way can life sprout anew, fresh, from his body the way water sprouts from the depths where it has been buried. And then he said that this was the meaning of becoming wise.

> *No power;*
> *a little knowledge;*
> *and as much flavor as possible…*

That being the occasion of his being inaugurated as a professor, he said that that's what he intended to be, from that moment on: a teacher of pleasure, one who is dedicated to teaching his young students the good taste of things! Anyone who makes a decision like that is affirming that pleasure is the only thing that is worthwhile. We live for pleasure. What's surprising is that that revelation was made as he was leaving behind his years of youth. Maybe wisdom is something crepuscular. I recall the words of Hegel, who said this in poetic form: "Minerva's owl spreads its wings only with the falling of dusk…"

There are people who manage to see right only with the arrival of old age. As you can see in these words erroneously attributed to Jorge Luis Borges: "If I could live my life again in the next life, I would try to make more mistakes. I would relax more. I would be even sillier than I've been. Truth is, I've taken very few things seriously. I'd contemplate more twilights, climb more mountains, swim more rivers, I'd start walking barefoot at the beginning of spring and I'd stay that way until the end of autumn. Because, in case you don't know, this is what life is made of, only moments. Don't miss the now."

These aren't words you'd expect from the mouth of someone old. No solemn warning. No serious advice. No dark word. Just the invitation to lightness. Life seen with an immense simplicity: a series of unexpected encounters with joy, which is always at hand. Ephemeral in its sunset colors, more delicious than a glass of wine or a kiss… Thus the advice: "don't miss the now." It will never happen

Joy

again.

Fernando Pessoa said the same thing in one of his poems:

A day when you didn't enjoy wasn't yours:
Your just withstood it.
Whatever you live
without enjoyment, you don't live.
You don't have to love, drink, or smile:
The sun's reflection on a puddle of water
is enough if it pleases you
Happy are those who, placing their pleasure
in the slightest things
have pleasure, are never denied
each day's natural fortune.

Very little is necessary. Joy is very near. It resides in the moment. We miss it because we think that it will come in the future, after some portentous event that changes our life.

But life: what is it? As Riobaldo said, "Life is the notion that people line up like this, but only by the law of a false idea. Each day is a day." And we go waiting for it to arrive after formation—of marriage, birth, travel, promotion, lottery, the election, the new house, the separation, the death of the husband. And it never gets there because joy doesn't live in the future but only in the now. It's there, shy and faithful, in the space of the house, in the space of the street. It we don't find it, it isn't life's fault. It's our fault. Our thoughts go far from the places where it lives, and that's why our eyes can't see it. As Mário Quintana said, "How many times we go off seeking our fortune but in vain, like old grandpa looking everywhere for the glasses that are on his nose."

Old age is when you realize that you can't expect a portentous event in the future, such as the beginning of happiness. But isn't this true of the whole of life? Maybe that's why the young should learn from the old that each day needs to be lived as if it were the last. Joy lives nearby. All you have to do to get it is effortlessly stick out your hand. But for that, it would be necessary for our eyes to be illuminated by the light of evening.

"Whether It's Good or Bad..."

When I used to tell my daughter stories—she was still small—there was a question she always asked me: "Did this story really happen?" I had no way to respond.

If Peter Pan were an adult, as he is in *Hook*, I would say right away that everything was just a little white lie of no importance that I had made up so she would go to sleep soon and I could go back to taking care of the important things in the real world of money, politics, work, the household chores. I would tell her that the book that was important to me was the one I was really reading, my bedside book, was the agenda with the green cover. In its pages was written reality. But she was *still* very much a child. In time she would grow and learn to read the literature of the real that can be read in agendas. *Meanwhile* she could surrender to

161

the lying words of stories, just so sleep might come more quickly...

But I wasn't the grown-up Peter Pan, and what I had to say I would not say because I thought it was too complicated for her bedside table. What I would like to tell her and did not tell her is that *the stories I was telling never happened so that they can always happen.* Neverland is the Alwaysland that exists eternally inside us. That which has in fact happened—documented, photographed, proven by science and written in the name of history—happened outside of us and therefore will never happen again. This death is buried in the past, and there is no spell that can bring it back to life. But that which never happened, that which was only dreamed, is that which has always existed and always will, that which was never born and will never die, and every time it's told, it happens again...

If she had asked me a different way, if she had asked me if I believed in the story, ah!—I would answered easily: "But of course I believe!" Because I only believe what never happened, in dreams, because it is dreams that we are made of.

The story of Snow White never happened, but all of us are, always, a stepmother who sees herself sad before the mirror and sends the girl—who, too, is us—to be killed in the forest. The story of Hansel and Gretel never happened, but in every child there is the terrible fantasy of abandonment. The story of Romeo and Juliet never happened, but we want to hear it again because inside of

162

us there is a dream of pure love, beautiful and immortal. And that's why I am incurably religious, because in the stories of religion, which never happened, the dreams and nightmares of the soul are reflected. I believe because I know they are a lie. If they were real, they would not interest me.

Stories are told like mirrors, so that we can discover ourselves. The orientals are great masters in this art, forgotten by occidentals because, like Peter Pan in the movie *Hook*, they grew up and went on to believe only in that which their agenda tells them, without noticing that, since it tells the truth, it lies.

I want to tell you the story that I have most told. It never happened. It always happens. A very rich man, upon his death, left his land to his sons. All of them got beautiful, fertile land, with the exception of the youngest, for whom was left a swamp that was useless for farming. His friends grew sad about that and visited him to lament the unfairness that had been done to him. But he said just one thing to them: "Whether it's good or bad, only the future can tell." In the next year, a terrible drought hit the country, and the land of his brothers was devastated. The springs dried up, the pastures grew parched, the cattle died. But the swamp of the youngest brother became a beautiful, fertile oasis. He became rich and bought a lovely white horse at a very high price. His friends organized a party because such a wonderful thing had happened. But they only heard one thing from him: "Whether it's good or bad, only the future can tell." The next day, his horse ran away, and his sadness was great. His friends came and lamented what had happened. But what the man said to them was the same words as always: "Whether it's good or bad, the future will tell." The next day, his son, without thinking, got on a wild horse. The horse bucked and threw him off. The boy broke a leg. The friends returned to lament the tragedy. "Whether it's good or bad, only the future will tell," the father repeated. A few days later, along came some soldiers of the king to take young men to war. All the boys had to go, minus the son with the broken leg. His friends celebrated and came to have a party. The father saw it all and said only one thing: "Whether it's good or bad, only the future can tell...."

Thus ends the story—with no end, just suspense. It could be continued indefinitely. And, as I tell it, it seems like the story of my life. My failures as well as my victories didn't last long. There is no professional or amorous victory that guarantees that life has finally resolved itself. No defeat could be a final condemnation. Victories are undone like sand castles touched by waves, and defeats turn into moments that proclaim a new beginning. As long as death does not touch us, since it alone is definitive, wisdom tell us that we always live at the mercy of unforeseeable accidents. "Whether it's good or bad, only the future can tell."

My Father's Pipe

had already planned to write about some other thing and was aiming for the computer with my outline in my hand when I smelled pipe smoke that left me longing. I thought it was strange because no one was smoking a pipe. Only my father. But he'd died a long time ago. It happens that my memory of him is preserved in a photograph that I put on my shelf. He is sitting in an armchair, his eyes lost in some indefinable place, his pipe in his mouth. He liked to smoke a pipe. Kind of bluish, spiraling and calm, the smoke invited daydreaming. My father was a dreamer. He smoked a pipe to dream. The curls of aromatic smoke that came from his pipe made me dream, too. The ideas I had been imprisoning on paper disappeared, and it made me feel like talking about things. Which isn't easy. I remembered Riobaldo, who knew that "telling is very difficult, not for the years that have passed but for the cleverness that certain past things have—to balance, to change all their places."

And he concluded: "The memory of our life gets stored in various stretches; some I think don't match up with others. Telling things in sequence, all lined up" (which was what I had planned), "only things of the least importance. There are old times that come closer to us than other more recent times. You yourself know, and you know, you understand me. All longing is a kind of old age."

Everything rearranged itself inside me with the smell of the smoke that came from my father's pipe in the photograph. I longed for him. I became old.

My father was very rich. Pretty much the owner of the world. When he was in his twenties, he was an exporter of coffee, had two cars, factories, farms, a cinema, several houses, money to do whatever he wanted. He had a problem with a street in our town that was very narrow. Because he was sure about it, he bought all the houses on one side of the street and knocked them down—just to realize his dream of widening the street. The street is still there, wide the way he made it. But then along came the crisis of 1930. He lost everything. Really everything. He even lost the house where we lived. We had to move to a house a brother-in-law lent him.

It was an old farm in Minas Gerais, one of those that doesn't have indoor plumbing, electric lights, a bathroom, or plastered walls, and at night you could hear the mice walking above the ceiling. My mother had to go get water out near the waterwheel. I will never forget the smell of the place, a smell that doesn't exist anymore and which still lives inside me with longing. I'm sad that I can't tell how it was. It wasn't really a smell. It was everything together: the water running in the irrigation ditches, the smell of green grass, the sound of the grist mill pounding. The smell of fermenting corn—a bad smell that's only good for memories like mine. At night, it was the smell of kerosene in the lamps. I have a painful memory of those times. Not far away was a wooded area, a compact and mysterious wall of trees. The grown-ups, just to make me suffer, said that a boy lived there all alone... "Want to see?" they asked. And through cupped hands they shouted, "Hey, boy!" And the echo answered in a disappearing voice, "Hey, boy..." I didn't know anything about echoes, and I imagined a boy like myself, lost and alone in the dark night of the woods. I was so sad I couldn't sleep...

I saw my father, a man used to the expensive things that money could buy, grab the handle of a hoe and the handle of a scythe, clothes soaking wet with sweat in the midday sun. But I never saw him depressed—something very strange for a man of 40 years who, having had everything, had to start over again with nothing, abandoned by his friends who used to smile and like him when he was rich. But, as Cecília says, "when the fall from grace is deep, which friend feels sorry for you?" I think my father had a rare, maybe crazy, capacity to find joy even in absolutely simple things. Maybe, if the roads of fate had been different, he would have been a poet. Because if you can believe Blake, this is what the soul of poetry is: "To see a world in a grain of sand and a Heaven in a wild flower..."

From those times of privation he had a memory that never abandoned him, and no matter how life's passages shifted around and balanced each other out, the memory always came back, and his face transfigured with joy when he retold it. When the sun was hottest out in the field and his sweaty body called for water, he purposefully put off that pleasure. He just imagined the fresh water running from the spring that was hidden in the shade of the trees. Only when the thirst turned intolerable did he go to the spring. And he described that unforgettable scene: kneeling on the moist earth before the clear water, dipping his mug into it to slake his thirst.

We moved from the farm to a little town that had a train. My father had decided to restart his life as a commercial representative, and as his days of automobiles were left behind, he would have to make use of the locomotive and second-class wagons. Our house...Ah! I remember that song: "It was a funny house, it had no roof, it didn't have anything. Nobody could come in because the house had no floor..." Well, roof and floor it had. But no table. We made our first table this way: My father took a door off its hinges and nailed it onto a crate that he got from a warehouse. It presented obvious problems with balance. If someone not paying attention rested an appendage on it, it moved like a seesaw and the food went flying. Knowing that food was in short supply, we were careful not to upset the table. But a friend who visited us, leaned on it in a moment of eloquence, and there went our lunch. The house didn't have a closet, either, just broomsticks across the corners of the walls.

Later things got better. We got dessert once in a while. Which was a party. Guaraná soda and ice cream, but only on special occasions, such as birthdays.

We moved to Rio. My father had a chance to get rich again. But it seems he wasn't born for that. The things that made him happy were very simple. To smoke a pipe... To see the rain falling on the plants and say, "look how they like it..." To sleep hearing drops of rain falling on a can. He dreamed of going back to the country to raise chickens. And he even tried that, but it was a failure. Because he never treated his chickens as possibilities for profit. He gave a name to each one and spent a lot of time contemplating them as they sought out their places to roost at the end of the day while he dreamed within the spirals of bluish smoke.

I missed him. And although it could be said that he failed, I admit I marvel at his mysterious power to find beauty and happiness in the simplest things in life. If there's a heaven, I hope it has hoes and scythes and that the sun is strong and that bodies get sweaty and that a spring lies hidden among the trees.

Birthday

My mother taught me that it isn't polite to ask people their age. I asked her why, but she wasn't able to give me reasons. I've never understood this rule of etiquette because I've never seen what's wrong with wanting to know something about the years of life that a person has accumulated. It was only a few weeks ago that I understood the good reasons hidden behind this taboo. It's that whatever the answer, it's always a lie. Even when the count is correct. Because this is how we get the answer: summing up the years that have passed from the year of birth to the year being lived now. If I say I have 58 under my belt, that number is obtained by adding up, one by one, the years that have gone by from the day of my birth in 1933 until today. The count is correct, but the answer is wrong. Because 58 years are precisely the years that I don't have. Fifty-eight is the number of years that have passed, years sunk in the past, years I can no longer count, years burned up and which will never burn again, like scratched matchsticks. The years of life don't add up. They subtract down.

So the correct question to be asked, especially on a birthday, isn't "How old are you?" but "How many years have you used up?" And the answers, to be true, would have to be in the form of "I've used up 25 years," "I've used up 37 years," "I've used up 72 years…"

Etiquette prohibits the terrible question because it obliges us to admit how much death we have accumulated in our body. Because the sum of years is actually the years of life that have been subtracted, the number of years that have died. The prohibition has its reason: behind the question about the years of life, what you're really asking about is the years of death.

The birthday liturgies surreptitiously announce the truth that etiquette wishes to hide. So much so that, to celebrate the occasion, we elect to blow out candles. There stand the candles on the cake, flames lit, the exact number of years lived. Here comes the birthday-boy, smiling and innocent, not really knowing what he's doing, and with a single puff blows out the candles. On the cake remain the charred wicks. Where there had once been flame, what's left of the light rises as a smear of black smoke. Everyone laughs, claps hands, and sings.

I admit I get stupefied, not noticing what's happening. But there's no way to deny it: the blowing out of candles is a symbol of death. Those are years that are dying. A candle blown out is a life gone by. I think that if we knew what was going on, we'd all have to weep and grieve.

Ah! Life, candle, fragile thing blown out with just one breath…

So I wonder if we shouldn't invert the ritual. In the dark and silent room a match is scratched, a candle lit—a candle that no breath will blow out and which will remain shining through the whole party. At the lighting of the candle, joy bursts out, not for the years lost but for those still waiting to be lived. Instead of blowing out the candle, the candle is lit…

And imagine if each person had a candle—their own candle, a candle not bought by the box, each unique, different from all the others. The candle would have to be made very slowly, drop by drop, following the rhythm of the body as it forms inside the body of the mother, cell by cell. Everyone who loves her can help. Everyone who wants can drip their melting wax on the body of the candle, making it grow on the outside while the little child is growing on the inside.

This candle would be more than a candle. It would be a prayer. It would have a story. It would have a name. Each candle is a desire of light and heat. Each candle is a recognition that, to produce light and heat, you have to not feel sorry for your own body. The candle lives by doing. Whoever makes a candle thinks about the beauty and sadness of life. And in this way, the candlemaker becomes more wise. And what more can you offer a child at birth than the wisdom of those already born? The candle would be evidence of the wishes of those already alive, offered to the one who is going to live. The wishes would say how life would be.

There are long, tall candles that wish to rise: winged dreams. Others, stout and round, are enchanted fruits: pleasure dreams. Luminous gifts for the eyes, perfumed gifts to delight the nose. What aroma is released as it burns? Cinnamon? Jasmine? Clove? Peach? Candles caress the body even when the eyes are closed. And their colors will be the colors of the wishes of those who made them. Because the soul is colorful...

And when the mother gives birth—gives light, as they say in Brazil—her child will cry the first tears of his or her life, and his or her candle will be lit, and it, too, will give light as the mother did, and will drip the first tear onto the melted wax that runs over his or her body.

With each birthday, the candle will leave its place, each time a little smaller, to be again lit, repeating the eternal lesson that, if it's true that life can be extinguished with a puff of wind, it is also true that it can be lit again if it is touched with a flame...

Writers and Cooks

I have a dream that I think I will never realize. I would like to have a restaurant. More precisely, I would like to be a cook. Kitchens are places that fascinate me, magic places. There pleasure is prepared. But to prepare pleasure, the cook must be a psychologist, a diviner of desires, a connoisseur of the secrets of body and soul. But I don't know how to cook. That's why I write. I write the way cooks cook. My head is a kitchen. The cook cooks thinking about the pleasure her art will produce in the one who eats. I write thinking about the pleasure my words can produce in one who reads.

The relation between cooking and writing has often been noted by writers. Etymology reveals the common origin of cooks and writers. In their origins, savor and savvy are the same thing. Once the Latin word sapare meant know and taste. Older Portuguese people remember that, in a Portuguese language no longer spoken, people could say

175

that food sabia bem—that it knew well. To know is to taste, to experience the taste of things: to eat them. The wise one is one who knows not only with the eyes but especially with the mouth. Anyone who knows something only with the eyes knows it from a distance because vision requires distance. Close up, you can't see anything. Anyone who knows with the mouth knows it from close up because you can only know the taste of what's already inside your body.

I suspect that Roland Barthes also had a secret envy of cooks. If he didn't, how to explain the astonishing revelation with which he ends one of his most beautiful works, The Lesson? He admits that for him the time had come to forget all the knowledge that had settled in by tradition and that now what interested him was "the most savoring possible." He wanted to write as one cooks—taking cooks as his teachers. He wanted to read the way one eats delicious food.

Mário Quintana also said that his dream was to produce with words something that would be good to eat and bring delight to the body:

I dream of a poem
whose juicy words slide
like the pulp of ripe fruit in the mouth,
a poem that kills you with love
Even before you know the mysterious meaning:
Enough to savor its taste...

176

The idea of eating suggests a delicious association. Because eating isn't only what happens at the table. Eating is also used to describe what happens in bed. To eat is to make love. The cook and the lover are motivated by the same desire: to please the other. The difference is that the lover offers the body itself to be eaten as an object of delight. The writer, like the lovers, also offers the body to the other as an object of pleasure, but in the form of words. Each writing is a eucharistic celebration. Eat, drink, this is my body..

Reading must be an experience of happiness. I desire the pleasure of my reader. Each reader, as Barthes suggested, imposes on the writer a condition for pleasure: "The text you write must give me proof of that which you desire for me." It is necessary that "words make love," as André Breton suggested. That's why Borges advised his students to only read texts that give them pleasure. "If the text pleases you, fine. If not, don't go on. Obligatory reading is something as absurd as obligatory happiness." You can't eat in obligation. You can't make love in obligation. You can't read with obligation.

That is the secret desire of every writer: the pleasure of the reader.

When I was traveling, I turned on the radio in my car and heard an ad for a course in dynamic reading: reading under the power of speed. That is the last thing a writer wants. Because pleasure requires time. Anyone having pleasure does not desire it to come to an end. Eating fast to finish soon? To make love fast to finish soon? Pleasure is lazy. It drags. It takes time. It wishes to stop to begin again.

And when it ends, it waits to do it again.

This is the reason I'd like to be a cook. It's easier to create happiness with food than with words... The cook knows his or her speciality dishes by heart. They've already been tested, approved, and enjoyed. It's enough to just do again what was done before. But that's exactly what is prohibited for the writer. The writer is a cook who every week must invent a new dish. Each week begins with anguish represented by the emptiness of three sheets of blank paper that give me an order: "Write something new here that gives pleasure!" To write is to suffer. Every pleasurable text tells a lie. It hides the pain of gestation and delivery. Once in a while someone says to me, "You write so easily!" I become happy. Someone admitted to me their pleasure in my words. But I know that that happiness only exists for the ones who read. The fire that burned me remained in the kitchen. Mário Quintana said you have to write several times in order to give the impression that the words were written the first time. Yes, so that they give the impression... Because if the writer's suffering appears, the words will have the taste of burnt food.

That's why each week I feel an enormous temptation to stop writing. To suffer less. Writing is cooking in which the cook always gets burned.

But it's worth getting burned for the joy in the face of one who eats the food you made.

Odyssey

"Want to become calm? Breathe softly before the light flame of a candle that does it light work softly."

Before I read this advice from Bachelard, I knew about the tranquilizing power of a small flame. The reason is that, among the useless things I surround myself with (useless because there's nothing I can do with them besides dream...) are candles. Once in a while I turn off the light in my living room, and there, in the silence, I awaken them from their patient and faithful sleep. Once lit, they set themselves to repeating the same things that they have always told me. They speak to me of life and death. They teach me wisdom. That's why I remain silent and listen.

I notice that the candle is a disciple of the twilight because the two tell me the same thing. Bachelard himself perceived: "The candle that goes out is a sun that dies.

The candle dies even more softly than the stars. The wick curls and darkens. From the darkness around it, the flame has taken its opium. And the flame dies well. It dies in its sleep." In the light surrounded by darkness, our thoughts are different.

Calm. Calm and lovely. Lovely and sad. Are you afraid of sadness? It would be better to befriend it. It's a cold counselor. I spent some time rereading the Scriptures and found in Ecclesiastes this strange suggestion: "It is better to go to the house of mourning than to go to the house of feasting: for that is the end of all men; sorrow is better than laughter: for by the sadness of the countenance the heart is made better."

To make the heart better is to become wiser. It's under the sad-lovely dusky light that life appears in its greatest clarity. Then we sense what the really important things are...

The erudite philosopher knew that wisdom is a gift of the twilight. At the end of his Philosophy of Right, at a moment of poesy, he said, "The owl of Minerva spreads its wings only with the falling of dusk." But, in a conclusion without hope, he says, "When it's too late. When there's nothing left to do...." For the disappointed philosopher, wisdom always arrives late. People become wise only after the moment of living has passed.

I don't agree. I think it's possible to learn the wisdom of the dusk while there's still time. That's the only reason I think and write. In his diaries of his youth this fragment can be found, certainly written in the evening: "If, during the day, the flight of birds always seems aimless, at night it would be said that they meet up with a purpose. They fly to something. So maybe in the night of life…"

Even young people can learn the lesson of the birds. At dusk their destination becomes clear in their flight. They no longer scatter through space. They go back to their place. The longing for the light of dusk tells us about our destination. We walk ahead to reencounter what the scattering of life, with its rushing around and delusions, made us lose. Bachelard meditated on this movement of the soul and felt that there was a longing for home: "Inside the familiarity where the candle and the candlestick unite, an indispensable pair in a residence of the old times, what is really desired is to return to a house we always return to, to dream and remember." The house to which we always return…

I don't like science fiction films about space travel. Too metallic and electronic for my taste. But there's an exception: 2001: A Space Odyssey. It's the saga of man's travel into the distant unknown, always farther away, to the stars, attracted by an enchanting music which calls out irresistibly from the emptiness like the sirens in the sea in Ulysses' odyssey. At the end of his long journey, the space traveller arrives at his destination: an unexpected place. No monsters or fabulous beings or unknown scenes. He finds himself in the dining room of a common house. Before him, a man with his back to him, seated at a table, eating breakfast. An ordinary, everyday domestic scene like so many he had lived. The unknown man, without saying a word, turns and faces him. His face is familiar. He knows him. It's he himself, transformed by the marks of years. He flew across endless space in search of the distant unknown. And now he sees that the objective of his search was very near, inside his own body.

A brusque movement and a crystal glass shatters on the floor. The scene changes. An old and agonizing man is seen on his deathbed. Again they hear the same mysterious sounds that had seduced him to travel so far. And the music turns into a vision: a starry sky in which floats, among the indifferent stars, a fetus, his eyes enormous, contemplating all in ecstasy.

The Odyssey is Ulysses's long journey back home to his love and his son, like the birds at dusk. The Odyssey in Space tells us that to go back home we need to stop being adults and again have the eyes of a child… Thus, "to the end of all our explorations we will arrive again where we started from and will then for the first time know…" (Eliot)

"Which road to take," Castañeda asked Don Juan, his sorcerer-teacher. "The road doesn't matter," he answered. "All roads lead to the same end. But choose the one road of love."

The end of the long odyssey back home isn't found at the end of the journey, like a triumphant conquest of work and profession. It is found at all points along the road. But only those with the eyes of children can see. That's why I love candles and the light of dusk. They make me forget I'm an adult.

"I'm Going Crazy..."

S^{he} arrived and, after a brief moment of indecision, said, "I think I'm going crazy…"

I remained silent, like a hunter waiting for the flight of the prey, because this is my profession. I am a hunter of words.

It was certain that some surprising change had occurred in her thoughts. Accustomed to tame, short-flight words that moved through her interior world every day, she must have been surprised at the sudden rising of another entity whose existence she had never suspected, hidden as it was in the shelter of the dense undergrowth that marks the edge of the obscurity of the soul. She had received the emissary of the unconscious—thoughts that she had never had, thoughts uncommon, unknown. She knew nothing of their origin nor of their destination. She had suddenly

183

found herself without solid ground under her feet, floating over the mystery. That's what she had told me with her statement: "I think I'm going crazy..."

But I didn't know anything about the color, the shape, or the movements of this mysterious bird that was scaring her. So I remained quiet, waiting... I confess that I felt a shiver of pleasure. Caged birds are always banal and can be bought anywhere. I don't pay them any attention since the newspapers and daily chit-chat are full of them. But these wild birds who announce themselves with the name *crazy* are born of the unknown and take us flying to other worlds where we have never been.

So, she continued, explaining what had happened. "I am a practical, uncomplicated person. I like to cook. And I do it competently, automatically, without thinking. I cut the onions, the chives, the tomatoes, and I go on doing the things that must be done in the way I have always done them. These things and these acts were never worth my attention. While I cook, my thoughts are focused on the final dish and in the pleasure of eating with friends.

"But, last week, something strange happened. I picked up an onion like all the others, cut a ring as I always did, and was surprised. I sensed that I had never seen an onion. Was that possible? I've seen and cut hundreds of onions, and now it was as if I were seeing the onion for the first time! I looked at the rounded shape, felt the smoothness

184

of its skin under my fingers, saw the rings, circular, perfect, one tucked into the next, the light fragmented in hundreds of shining points on its surface. My practical, unconscious thought was interrupted. I left the knife on the sink and was spellbound with the onion ring in my hand. I forgot about the dish I was preparing. At that moment, I didn't want to make any dish whatsoever for the delight of the mouth, because I had encountered another form of delight: the delight of the eyes. My eyes were eating the onion ring. And I sensed a pleasure I had never before sensed.

"For the first time in my life I saw that the onion is beautiful. If I were a painter, I would paint an onion. If I were a photographer, I would photograph an onion... My onion had left behind being just a creature from the produce section of the supermarket, at the mercy of knives and chewing jaws, and it seemed like an enchanted creature, resident of the world of beauty, beside jewels and works of art.

"When I awoke from the mystic trance, where I saw an onion ring as if it were a stained glass window in a Gothic cathedral, I became frightened. What strange thing must have happened to my eyes? What strange transformation must have been happening to me?

"If I told my friends what had happened, they would not understand. They would think that I was kidding. They would laugh. I had to remain silent about my experience.

Then I thought that I was going crazy. Because craziness must be this: that which you experience and have to keep quiet about. Because if you talk about it, others will not understand and will start to think that you've got a screw loose.

"But the worst is that what happened with the onion began to happen with everything. My eyes were no longer the same. They were possessed of a new psychedelic power. They saw what they'd always seen in a way they'd never seen. My paintings became different. My things became different. My plants became different. And most disturbing was the silly happiness that I sensed in everything. And I thought, if I keep feeling happy like this, all of my big plans will fall to the ground. If I feel joy at the smallest things, I'll stop struggling to accomplish big things…."

She was frightened of happiness. She was scared to sense that joy resided nearby. Seeing was enough. And I told her: "You aren't going crazy. You are becoming a poet…."

The poetic experience isn't the seeing of grand things that no one sees. It's seeing the absolutely banal that is in front of our noses…in a different light. When this happens, each daily thing is transformed into the entrance of an enchanted world. And you can begin a journey without leaving your place…. We find what we're looking for right before our eyes. You don't have to do anything.

I'm Going Crazy

You don't have to travel to distant places. Is there anything
more useless than a trip when your eyes see everything
in black and white? It also isn't necessary to accomplish
great feats of struggle and work—because beauty can be
found within reach. Blake said: "To see a world in a grain of
sand and a heaven in a wild flower..." No, she wasn't going
crazy. But I understood her fright. She had discovered the
poetic. And the craziness of poetry is precisely in this:
the understanding that it's enough for beauty to reside
within the eyes so that the interior world is transfigured by
them. Happiness is born from within the eye that has been
touched by poetry.

Bullshit and Politics

One look was enough to know he was up to something... His face was that of a mature man, but his shifty smile said that inside resided a brat who had just committed some kind of art...art in both senses: the artifice of a brat and the creation of an artist. Because that's what he was. In the end, there isn't a whole lot of difference between the two.

The brat as much as the artist does what reality does not allow. I remained quiet, waiting to hear what he had to say.

"I have been contracted to decorate a space. I walked around, looking up, waiting for inspiration to come to me from on high. But one who looks up doesn't see where he's going. As a result, I stepped in a cow pie. I got mad. My boot sunk into that malodorous green pasta. But my anger soon passed as my eyes discovered delicate details in that work that an unpleasant contraction at the end of a ruminant's alimentary canal had produced without needing any special inspiration.

"I looked around and found similar works already dried in the sun, which allowed for a more detailed inspection— to the point of actual manipulation with no great danger. And thus I was crouched in scatological contemplation of the aesthetics of cow shit when inspiration came to me... In a fraction of a second I saw the work of art I was going to produce.

"I collected a pile of the most beautiful bovine turds, carefully took them to my atelier (there was always the danger of such fragile things to break). I spray-painted them gold and tied them together with clear nylon string. I turned them into mobiles that floated in space...

"People came along and stopped, looked and were enchanted. 'Such lightness,' they said in admiration. Then they asked me about the technique I used in fabricating those golden metallic discs. But of course I didn't say anything. I kept my secret..."

And he fell down laughing. And so did I.

A laugh is a sudden ejaculation of joy. And it happens when the unexpected appears before us and trips us up. Every good joke-teller knows this. The punchline has to be an ending that no one was expecting. It's the unexpected wit that makes the body explode in laughter.

190   A laugh reveals one of the secrets of the soul. The soul doesn't like to march. In a march, everything is equal, predictable, done in a military parade. The soul is a ballerina

that likes most to dance. And that's why, in its original state (and this is the lesson that psychoanalysis teaches us), the soul is a playful child. It's a sorceress who delights in the most unheard-of and prohibited transformations. It's a poet who writes, and the world is never the same. It's a clown who laughs because the world is so much like a circus...

And that's what my friend was at that moment: a boy, an artist, a dancer, a clown, a sorcerer who puts a bull flop on his hat and, abracadabra, the hat turns into floating gold. This was the secret that the alchemists wanted to discover. But, poor things, they were looking in the wrong place, in complicated laboratories without knowing that anyone can make this magic happen.

It's been a while since that happened, but all of a sudden I recalled (nice word, that one, wanting to say "call again" that which has been kept in the heart...). Because it was children who made me go back to the heart, children and adolescents, kids going somewhere, singing and following the song. I never imagined that I would ever see this again, black clothes, the color of mourning, gloomy and harsh, feces, excrement, who could it be who made them dress this way: But their faces spoke otherwise, faces painted, joy, hope, jokes, laughs...

Sometimes very strong magic is needed to awaken Sleeping Beauty! Sometimes you need a lot of shit to make the unconscious soul awaken from its sleep and say, "This is not what I am! I am Beauty! I am a golden floating mobile! I am a flower!"

In no way similar to political parties with their flags, their erected fingers, their rasping throats, their mottos and commands, the outpourings of youth were pure explosions of life, laughs, ejaculations of joy before the unexpected, the unexpected being that Beauty still exists despite the malodorous excrement leaving the end of the insatiable alimentary canal of the powerful.

Neruda said once that poets (those bad politicians) began the happiness revolution. So I think that this is what the young are proclaiming: that in the middle of shit (pardon this word, but no other does justice to the reality!) it is possible for a flower to sprout. Because, as everyone knows, cow shit, after composting for a while, is good manure. We can make a garden with the excrement of the powerful....

About Rubem Alves

Rubem Alves (1933—2014) was a theologian, philosopher, educator, psychoanalyst, and one of Brazil's most popular writers. Born in Boa Esperança, Minas Gerais, he went on to earn a Ph.D. from Princeton Theological Seminary. He also trained and practiced as a psychoanalyst. His most recent professorship was at the Universidade Estadual at Campinas. He is the author of hundreds of essays and 40 books on pedagogy, theology, philosophy, and life in general. His works have been published in 13 countries and translated into various languages. More information is available at the Instituto Rubem Alves in Campinas, São Paulo State, Brazil (www.rubemalves.com.br).

About Raquel Alves

Raquel Nopper Alves is the youngest of three children of Rubem Alves. With her birth, his view of the world changed. He began to write only that which would come from his heart.

Raquel earned an undergraduate degree in landscape architecture and urbanism and Master's degree in Urbanism before working 15 years as a landscape architect. And just as her birth transformed the life of the writer, the death of her father in 2014 transformed her, too. She carries within her the fruit of seeds he nurtured. For that reason, she gave up landscape architecture and became director and president of the Instituto Rubem Alves, which was founded to disseminate and eternalize the work and legacy of the writer.

About the Translator

Glenn Alan Cheney is a translator, writer, and editor in Hanover, Conn. His more than 25 books explore myriad topics, including Brazil, nuns, Chernobyl, nuclear issues, the Pilgrims, Abraham Lincoln, Gandhi, bees, and Swaziland, as well as novels, stories, poems, and essays. He is the founder and managing editor of New London Librarium. He lives in Hanover, Conn. with his wife, Solange Aurora.

Acknowledgements

The translator and publisher owe special thanks to Raquel Alves and the Instituto Rubem Alves for permissions, assistance, and a finme foreword. Special thanks go to senior editors Ralph Hunter Cheney and Denise Dembinski for their suggestions and corrections.

www.ingramcontent.com/pod-product-compliance
Lightning Source LLC
Chambersburg PA
CBHW021845090426
42811CB00033B/2144/J

* 9 7 8 0 9 9 8 5 4 3 6 2 8 *